A Garden Well Placed

The Story of Helmingham and Other Gardens

This book is dedicated to Tim, to Selina and James,
Edward and Sophie, James and Florrie, and to my grandchildren,
Ralph, Theo, Lily, Sylvie, Stella and Minna.

A Garden Well Placed

The Story of Helmingham and Other Gardens

XA TOLLEMACHE

Pimpernel
Press LTD
www.pimpernelpress.com

Contents

PAGE 2: Early Dutch honeysuckle
(*Lonicera periclymenum* 'Belgica')

PAGES 4–5: Flora in the Rose Garden, flanked by 'Albéric Barbier' standard roses

Pimpernel Press Limited
www.pimpernelpress.com

A Garden Well Placed
The Story of Helmingham and Other Gardens

A catalogue record for this book is available from the British Library.

Design by Becky Clarke Design
Typeset in Utopia

ISBN 978-1-910258-80-4
Printed and bound in China
By C&C Offset Printing Company Limited

9 8 7 6 5 4 3 2 1

FOREWORD

BY FERGUS GARRETT

Xa Tollemache is an innately sensitive designer, combining classical and contemporary styles with a deep and perceptive understanding of the sense of place. She reads the scene so beautifully well, embracing the qualities of history, landscape, architecture, and people, within her work. She then balances this with her own creativity and individual style to produce designs which have their own distinct character but also embody the setting and the essential virtues of the site.

Xa's creations are utterly charming, wholly romantic, flowing and overspilling with flowers, all set within a framework of formality. She paints with plants, her designs placing a great emphasis on flowers with beautifully blended colours, pulling on years of experimentation and observation in her own garden at Helmingham Hall. The gardens here are testament to her style: you lose yourself in a world of classical parterres flanked with Hybrid Musk roses, colourful perennial and mixed borders, topiary and formal hedges, tunnels of sweet peas, climbing roses on wires surrounding rows of vegetables, with wilder areas around the edges. At Helmingham, you are seduced by vistas and drawn along grass paths tempting you into one space after another, each compartment different but all linked seamlessly in their design and all sitting within the embrace of a deer park studded with grand trees amongst pasture, blending into the surrounding Suffolk countryside. Her ideas fine-tuned over years of experience within the masterpiece of Helmingham, Xa's flair has resulted in the most sophisticated, multi-dimensional, and considerate designs.

There are direct similarities between the garden I work in, Great Dixter, and Helmingham, both with great houses wrapped by grounds dripping with flowers. Both are set within strong formal bones of hedges, walls, and topiary and both have an intimate connection to the countryside beyond. Like Great Dixter, Helmingham is alive with wildlife, just as any good garden should be. Pyramidal and marsh orchids, willow emerald damselflies, turtle doves, little owls, spotted flycatchers, pygmy shrews and much more show the diversity there is within a mosaic of nectar- and pollen-rich borders, ancient buildings, porous walls, old orchards, and long grass. All of this is a consequence of years of nurture and sensitive and careful management resulting in an abundance of biodiversity. Our own biodiversity audit at Great Dixter showed the garden to be far richer and more diverse than the land around it. This is the case at Helmingham too, and significantly this aspect of our gardening becomes critically important as biodiversity is increasingly under pressure, and gardens especially, have a part to play in the joint effort – being kinder to the planet.

INTRODUCTION

Before we look at the gardens I have designed, in various stages of undress and then in their final glory, I want to explain my philosophy about garden design.

First of all, of course, comes Helmingham and my life there from 1975 to 2017.

I am passionate about plants but I understand that a garden doesn't work without a coherent design. It needn't look designed but it has to make sense. I feel the undesigned garden is like a picture that isn't mounted or framed or indeed hanging in the right place. Design is a method by which plants work. Having said that, plants growing naturally in the wild are in their own design, which in my view is far more beautiful than any human-crafted garden.

When I am asked to design a garden, I am instantly excited. Whether it is a country garden, town garden, a seaside garden, a historic garden or a cottage garden. I always have to think about lots of things. First, I must consider the 'place'. Alexander Pope, the philosopher, poet, garden designer and all the rest, said, 'Consult the genius of the place in all.' I have learned that good design is a personal thing and that the place where we are must please both the client and the designer. The ultimate celebration of the place looks at the surrounding landscape, the architecture of the house and, of course, the people who are living there and what are their interests, likes and dislikes.Living, working and observing at Helmingham taught me those vital and essential elements.

In some of my designs I use the Golden Mean (the mathematical formula for perfect proportion and therefore balance and harmony), although it might not be obvious. Scale, balance and proportion are vital elements. But it isn't easy. Landscape and garden design are not just the most physically expressive of all the art forms, they are the ones that grapple with the notion of time and place. I was told once that we are completely ruled by the sun, the moon and the seasons; we are not in control. Anyone who gardens consistently will understand this.

It might be said that the destination of our culture is dependent on our relationship with nature and the ancient art of gardening is the obvious expression of that link with the world we live in. This has never been more poignant than now, with our ever-changing climate.

* * *

A buff-tailed bumblebee (*Bombus terrestris*) on *Allium cristophii*

Now, I have to say that I am not a trained garden designer, I have not taken a degree in landscape architecture, nor have I done a course in garden history. I have not even completed, actually never started, a course of garden design in any of those first-class establishments.

Anybody, certainly any designer, has every right to call me an amateur. (They did, actually, at Chelsea, but I did get a Gold Medal.) I don't know how to build a wall, I have not mastered the technique of axonometric or perspective drawing. I freak out if anyone mentions a CAD or vector works software. I also have to admit to a lack of knowledge about drainage. But what I lack in professional knowledge, I think I gain in a sort of freedom, unrestricted by the golden rules of garden design and their disciplines.

Of course I have made mistakes, but I don't make them twice. I have a brilliant assistant who gained Distinctions in absolutely everything and I rely heavily on my trusted contractors, who do know how to build a wall. Another plus is that I have gardened. I learnt what the soil felt like in my hands, I dug and double dug. I studied plants and where they should go. I tried out at Helmingham combinations that pleased me. (I freely admit that some were accidental, but I can now present them as original ideas.) Some were disasters but my ultimate pleasure was in handling the plants, feeling how robust or how fragile they were, how deep they had to be planted – and then my astonishment when they actually grew!

I will discuss my garden education when I talk about Helmingham, but I can say that I am now a qualified and professional designer, having passed the very stringent Society of Garden Designers exams, which I thought were far harder than my 11-plus, or my GCE in maths, or my first Grand Prix dressage test on my horse (and that's saying something). So I have MSGD after my name.Of course, if I had been trained . . .

I don't know what part of the exercise of designing a garden gives me most pleasure. The initial tinkling with my pencil on a blank sheet of paper, seeing the design in its rawest state but knowing the bones of the plan are on the right track. Then the planting plan, which is always high up there on excitement. However, I really think what is most exciting is arriving at a site, seeing all the trolleys being unloaded, placing the trees, putting the structure plants in place and then the ultimate joy of planting. The tidying of the soil and perhaps a mulch complete the process.

When I am planting a border, it often changes from the plan. When I have plants in my hand it's as if I am painting a picture in my head.

I think I am terribly lucky to have had the chance of a career relatively late in life. My husband was so thrilled when I gave up dressage and started designing gardens. (It meant money coming in rather than going out!) I really feel that most of my clients have become friends, and if they had a gardener, then he or she became a friend too. I love working alongside a team of people who are similarly enthusiastic and excited, so that I can feel positive that the garden will be well looked after when I leave it.

Me in my favourite wheelbarrow

HELMINGHAM HALL

SUFFOLK

ABOVE: A red deer stag in the park

Helmingham sits serenely in an ancient deer park and as you come in past the lodges and drive through an avenue of ancient oaks planted in around 1680, you are only gradually introduced to this fine, warm red-bricked house surrounded by its wide moat. It is firmly anchored in this gentle countryside under the huge Suffolk skies so admired by artists.

The Tollemache family has lived in Suffolk from shortly after the Norman Conquest to the present day. It seems certain that the family came over from Avranches in Normandy and their surname was spelt Talemache, meaning Purse Bearer. Indeed, it was recorded that Hugh Talemache was Purse Bearer to King Henry I. (Although some Tollemaches have claimed that 'Before the Normans into England came, Bentley was my seat and Tollemache my name', this was just a boast, thought to be untrue.)

John Tollemache lived north of Ipswich at Bentley. He married Elizabeth Joyce, the heiress of Helmingham, where the family home of Creke Hall stood. They pulled down Creke Hall and started building Helmingham Hall in 1487. Work on the house was finished in 1510 and then the gardens were laid out, growing fruit, vegetables and flowers.

OPPOSITE: 'Iceberg' roses at the entrance to the Walled Garden

LEFT: The upper ley beside the garden moat
BELOW: The Oak Avenue

Ever since, the house has been lived in by generations of Tollemaches up to the present family. We brought up our children here and the shouts and laughter of our grandchildren now resound through the house as they tear around the corridors.

Old plans and maps show that the original shape of the old Walled Garden predates the house and is probably Saxon in origin and that it was enclosed by a garden moat, which served the purpose of protecting stock from marauders. There was a wooden palisade which was used to protect the garden from the deer until the garden walls were built and the fine cedar of Lebanon trees planted, in 1745. I like to think that the garden has been manured for over a thousand years.

The wider estate includes a long-established in-hand farm and a number of tenant farmers, some of whose families have farmed the land longer than Helmingham has stood.

The house itself was originally built in traditional half-timbered style with an overhang to the upper floor both to the outside and inside the courtyard and has had many changes during the centuries, but its basic form of a courtyard manor house has never altered.

People are always fascinated by the brick chimneys, many of which are original and each one slightly different, although all have had to be repaired over the last two centuries. The Bulmer Brick and Tile Company holds prototypes of each individual brick and mould, so, when necessary, they are able to reproduce the original design.

In 1760 there were several changes and the gables were removed, save for the ones at the corners. The half-timbered walls were concealed with brick on the lower walls and mathematical tiles on the upper walls. These clay tiles are only 6 mm/¼ inch thick, and they are hung by wooden pegs. They were probably first introduced in the seventeenth century to update and weatherproof old timber-clad buildings. They provide the structural lightness that brick doesn't have and were used here to enhance the façade of the house to match the conventional brick walls. I was told one day that this Hall is one of the largest areas where these tiles were used.

The great Regency architect John Nash was asked by Wilbraham Tollemache in around 1800 to cover the façade with grey stucco and add battlements, as he thought this would make the house look grander and more like a castle. (Thank heavens this didn't last; it was removed about twenty years later.)

Over the centuries, there have been three Tollemaches who have made huge differences to the house, and they were all called John.

The first John built the house in 1487 but three and a half centuries later, in 1840, another John, the first Lord Tollemache, finding the house in a pitiful condition, did major restoration work on the west side, removing a small garden leading off from the dining room, thereby making this room much bigger, heightening its walls and also those of the drawing room and the main bedrooms above them. It is believed that the famous Victorian architect Anthony Salvin did this work.

I would imagine this was very necessary, as Lord John had twenty-four sons and a daughter! One of his two wives produced sixteen children. John could have had a full cricket team of Tollemaches; however, only twelve actually achieved full maturity.

This enlargement and improvement to the Hall has over the years been invaluable, as there are now decent rooms for large-scale entertainment and for holding charity functions, the rest of the house having comparatively small rooms.

Just over a hundred years later, in 1953, the third John, my father-in-law, inherited the house from a cousin and again found the hall in a state of neglect (although the gardens were always maintained). Inside the house there was no running water (the inhabitants drank the moat water, and lived to a ripe old age), no electricity, no bathrooms, the roof had many holes and there were bricks and tiles lying around in piles. It is said that an old relative, Aunt May, who lived in the house in three rooms, sat in the sitting room with an umbrella over her head.

In 1953, when they started work renovating the Hall, in order to get electricity installed, my father-in-law had to turn the coach house into a dairy and buy some dairy cows. As it was necessary for the milking parlour to have electricity, they were then allowed to get power into the Hall.

He and my mother-in-law, Dinah, had the courage, the determination and the energy to completely restore the house to become a family home once more. They had four sons; my husband, Tim, was eleven years old when they finally moved in. It is entirely thanks to them that we were able to live there and bring up our children, just as our son and his family can now.

It would be absolutely impossible to do that degree of restoration and repair in the present day and without it

Helmingham would probably have been pulled down, as so many houses were after the war. Fortunately, every few centuries Helmingham has had a saviour who loved the house and was determined to save it. (Lucky us!)

Although safely restored back into a family home once more, it was still perishingly cold, with no central heating. One memorable weekend there were Danish friends staying and, being used to their well-heated houses, they were freezing. The wife came down to breakfast and described scraping the ice off from inside the windows with her highly polished nails. They remarked that however much they loved my parents-in-law, they could never come back!

To reach the house there are two drawbridges over the house moat that have to be negotiated. I remember the thrill the first time I visited Helmingham as a very young girl, as I crossed one of the drawbridges into the courtyard. The main drawbridge takes arriving cars into the courtyard and the back drawbridge is a footbridge. They have both been pulled up every night since 1510, to make Helmingham into a very secure island.

Before my time, both drawbridges had to be pulled up by hand, involving a heavy chain and turning handle. One night a group of fairly merry young men came home late and one of the visiting boys bravely took on this job, with the result that it sprang back and the poor boy was carted off to hospital with a broken arm. It was then decided to switch the operation of raising and lowering the drawbridges to electric power.

There was an amusing occasion when the insurance firm came to visit, claiming that it wasn't as secure as they had been told. So, John put the drawbridges up just before they arrived and watched in great amusement as they walked right round the Hall trying to get in. Eventually he pulled the drawbridge down. There were no more queries about security after that!

Unfortunately, John died in 1975, when he was only sixty-six years old. Dinah went to live on their Cheshire estate in a warm farmhouse and we moved into Helmingham. We had married in 1970 and it had taken two years to restore Framsden, one of the farmhouses on the estate, and so we only had three happy years there before moving.

By then our daughter, Selina, had arrived and I was pregnant with Edward. As I felt very ill most days, it wasn't an easy process to pack up our beloved Framsden and move into a rather icy Helmingham.

Helmingham Hall, with the
drawbridge half-raised

I think both Tim and I felt very dubious and sad at leaving our farmhouse but, with the vigour and optimism of youth, we got down to the task of making the Hall our special family home. The first winter seemed very bleak and we had to put Selina into a makeshift bedroom which was the warmest one available. Edward was born the following May. It was a very hot spring and I remember pulling one of Tim's shirts over my large pregnant tummy and lowering myself into the moat to cool off. After a nice swim I came out, and, as the moat was rather weedy, I had a shower to de-slime myself. As I was drying off by the window, I saw this enormous fish with whiskers rise up, just where I had been swimming. I rushed downstairs and asked Tim what it could have been. He replied, 'Oh, that must be Danny the catfish, I thought he had died.' After that Danny was often seen. He caused much curiosity among young children and also provided a helpful deterrent to keep them from going too near the moat (and falling in!). He was put in the moat by my father-in-law and lived for about sixty years.

James, our third child, arrived in 1980 to complete our family.

One of the first things I did was to create a nursery wing from the old servants' living quarters on the first floor. As we didn't have any live-in staff, I had a blank canvas to play with. The rooms were sparse with very thin carpets and a runner down the passage with bare floorboards on either side. It was extremely dreary and freezing in winter. However, despite the deficient heating, we filled the house with friends and their young children.

After living in the house for a couple of years, we started to think about some redecoration. In 1978 a friend recommended David Mlinaric, who was well known but not the iconic figure he became later, restoring and redecorating many of the great houses in the UK, including the Royal Opera House, Covent Garden.

Luckily, he lived locally. He came over one day and suggested that we move all the furniture and rehang the pictures correctly before doing any decorating in the house. We also rewired half of the house at a time and lived in the other half when doing this. We started with the main guest bedrooms and our bedroom and bathrooms, then moved down to the little sitting room under the nursery wing, which is where we wanted to sit in the evenings. Slowly moving round, a year at a time, David then suggested redecorating the big drawing room.

The moat banks in spring are thick with daffodils

It has the most splendid French mohair velvet curtains which he said would cost a fortune to replace, if, indeed, you could find the quality again. He very sensibly suggested relining them. As a result, they are still in place and look wonderful with their original tassel ropes. The walls were a very dull cream and very tainted with cigar and cigarette smoke.

David had worked for the Duchess of Devonshire at Lismore and had found and had reprinted a Pugin wallpaper and thought we could have the same pattern but in another colour, the drawing room being of the same Victorian era. Debo Devonshire gave us her consent, but this wallpaper came with a huge pattern and I was afraid it would dominate this room with all its historic pictures. In the end I chose a colour of the background sky in one of the pictures, a dusky pale pinky brown. David assured us that it would work and of course it did. The room and its beautiful furniture and pictures were transformed. He also sent me a swatch of a French blue chenille for the two huge sofas. I said it looked like a Sloaney old woman wearing a tweed skirt with a Husky jacket and leading a golden retriever. He tried some others, then came back saying, 'Look at the tweed skirt again.' I did and it proved to be the perfect colour in the drawing room. He had an extraordinary sense of what was right for Helmingham, at the same time making it cosy and comfortable.

His timeless classical elegance still looks wonderful nearly forty years later. I think my son and daughter-in-law agree that the main rooms look not at all dated, which is a testament to his appreciation of the house and superb knowledge of doing it right. He used to say to me, if I boldly suggested something, that 'it's nice, but not as nice as nice can be.'

During this work to the house and in the following years, I learned to do almost every job, whether it was spring cleaning, washing all the china in the cabinets, cleaning the panelled dining room (using vinegar and water before putting good-quality polish on), or learning to cook. I then appreciated the beautiful things in the house and could knowledgeably ask other people to do these important jobs. I know how long it takes to make up one of the large double beds and to turn a mattress. (I remember one day I came into the dining room to find my much-loved local daily up a ladder with a tin of Pledge, thinking she would give the very early Tudor portraits 'a bit of a shine'. Luckily, I persuaded her that perhaps there were better ways.) I learned how long it would take to cook a dinner party and get it unspoiled to the dining room. It was all a good education in getting to know how the house worked in every aspect.

Over the years we were both very heavily involved in various charities and we hosted many charity events. One of the first things we did was to have a staff party, bringing together everyone who worked in the house or in the garden, on the farm or in the woodlands. This had not been done before, and we were very raw and ignorant about what people would be happy and comfortable with.

Our agent's wife kindly agreed to make a pâté, beautifully decorated with delicate goodies. We had asked great friends to come for the whole of Christmas and they decided to take their children to Norwich to get out of our way as I madly cooked and prepared for this party. But their dog, Finn, was left behind and, to my horror, I found him scraping the top of the pâté with his claws and relishing it very much! I broke up some crisps and smoothed it over and hoped that the creator of this culinary wonder didn't notice.

Of course, the party was a complete disaster, with the various teams keeping to themselves and not mixing with anybody and hating all the fussy food I had cooked. We persevered and eventually, a few years later, we were able to give a great, relaxed party with everyone at ease and mixing happily.

I am a fresh air fiend and growing up in the country, we had a very free childhood. My sister and I would think nothing about getting on our ponies and disappearing for most of the day. I was probably no more than eight years old, and my sister two years older.

Of course, nowadays that would be unthinkable. However, we did bring our children up to be self-sufficient and, despite nervousness about the moat and the ponds around the house, I used to tell them to go out after breakfast and I would ring the bell when it was time for lunch. This meant they made up their own games and made dens and mud slides, an added value to living in the country. We both felt that this was an important lesson for them – not to be reliant on adults to provide all the entertainment. Now Selina, Ed and James are all wonderful parents themselves.

I became President of the local Riding for the Disabled and I had a fun day at Helmingham every year, including holding a camp when all the ponies came to Helmingham, creating much fun and excitement and utter exhaustion after it. There was a local group who would meet three times a week and we were very honoured when Her Royal Highness The Princess Royal came to visit us twice. The smiles on the children's faces told us everything.

There were also traditions that I took over from my mother-in-law and one of them was to give the Helmingham Primary School a Christmas party every other year. This meant booking an entertainer, giving the children a huge tea (with crackers) and then buying presents according to their age and gender and wrapping them so that Father Christmas could come and sit under the tree to give them out.

To start with, in the early 1980s, there were nineteen children. By the time I gave my last one, there were seventy-three. It had become an extremely expensive tea party! I still meet people, now parents themselves, who remember my parties. I had to be pretty organized to arrange this so near Christmas, so the supermarket visit was made in late November.

Another charity I got involved with in the early 1980s was the newly formed Ormiston Families. This looks after young people in the eastern region who are at risk or disadvantaged. It has grown into a most amazing charity and I am just as heavily involved with it after nearly forty years.

Being a keen rider, I used to compete in events and then Team Chasing, which was a fairly dangerous hobby. So when my sister introduced me to dressage, Tim was very relieved that at least I wasn't risking life and limb (and leaving three young children for him to look after). Dressage took up a great deal of time over the next ten years, although the competing was strictly in term time, and I was lucky enough to have two good horses which got me up to the top level of Grand Prix. Eventually, when these two horses retired, I realized I wasn't good enough, young enough or rich enough to continue, and it was then that I started my garden design business.

Tim, meanwhile, was running the farm and estate and then became Lord Lieutenant for Suffolk, a distinguished position in the county. He performed excellently in this role, and was very highly thought of.

But he is a countryman at heart and passionate about the countryside and the preservation of it. In the early years he planted miles and miles of hedges, where previously there were huge flat fields and the emphasis was on growing food for everyone. Tim was the first generation to really think about husbandry of the estate, retaining all the sheep-droving meadows, creating wetlands (which are a haven for wild duck and geese, and in the winter teal, widgeon and migrating snipe find there a safe haven), preserving wildlife by having field margins and managing the hedgerows to allow their growth for nesting birds. He has made nesting boxes for barn owls and by our barn for the swifts. He is very knowledgeable about wild flowers, inheriting this passion from his mother, and he manages the ancient woodlands to let in the light necessary for encouraging wild orchids.

He has won awards for his schemes and for running this estate in a sensitive way for the environment. Among all his patronages while Lord Lieutenant, he has retained being President of the Suffolk Wildlife Trust, which does such a valuable job in the county.

Many years later, I was thinking of what to give Tim on his seventieth birthday and came up with the idea of a beautiful picture of Helmingham, something which had not been done before. Some friends had commissioned a Frenchman called Jean-Marc Winckler. I greatly admired his style and the joyous way he had interpreted their houses. So I got hold of him and asked him to come over from Paris to have a look at Helmingham. The painting had to embrace the surroundings of Helmingham and the park which Tim had so assiduously looked after, with its herds of red and fallow deer and ancient oak trees.

The only problem was that it had to be kept a secret. So, whenever Tim told me he was going fishing, whether to Scotland or Iceland or Russia, we arranged for Jean-Marc to come over or for me to go to Paris to look at the picture. (It must have seemed very suspicious when I whizzed off to Paris whenever Tim left the house.) Getting it back and finding the right framer and then placing it in the best place tested the efficiency of our secrecy and finally, with the help of the children, we were able to hang it during his birthday dinner.

The whole family had generously contributed to the picture and so all Tim's brothers and their families were present. We led him into the boudoir, all lit with candles and there was this amazingly beautiful picture. He was rendered speechless.

Jean-Marc Winckler, *Helmingham Hall*, 2009

Dear Jean-Marc was a character. He had learned his English from *The Wind in the Willows* and could quote great reams of it and sing little French songs in-between. We made great friends and I loved arriving in his garret on the top floor of an old Parisian house, with the picture being shown off on his bed and the kitchen dishes all piled up with last night's tins of food hanging around.I believe the Rothschild family supported this penniless artist, asking him to paint all their houses, and thus his reputation grew and he was able to create a living from his commissions.

This picture remains, quite rightly, at Helmingham, to mark our forty-two years there. It was in 2013 that we all decided Tim and I would leave the house four years later, in 2017. (I believe we are the family to have lived at the house for the longest period.)

We tried to leave the estate in good shape. The house and garden have been put on a commercial level, opening for four days a week, hosting big events and plant fairs and introducing weddings, so that Edward and Sophie can take Helmingham on into the future. We count ourselves very fortunate that they have taken up the estate so enthusiastically and efficiently, and we have every confidence that it will continue to thrive.

THE GARDENS

When the house was completed in 1510 they started work on the gardens, laying them out in a similar fashion to what they are now, with fruit, vegetables and flowers along grass paths. The actual shape of the Walled Garden predates the house by many years. It is thought that going back to Saxon days, when the original house was there, livestock were kept within the garden moat.

Before 1745, when the present walls were built and eight cedars of Lebanon planted, a wooden palisade kept the deer from entering the garden (We have lost five of the eight original cedars of Lebanon, as they only have a lifespan of 250 years.)

There are two main gardens at Helmingham: the original garden, on the west side, and the more recent garden, which was laid out in 1982, on the east. The intention here was to create something historically sympathetic to the house; we wanted it to look something like a garden that the family might have seen in Tudor times.

BELOW: The main border, leading up to the Hall
OPPOSITE: Mungo and me

A NEW BEGINNING

I was little more than a young bride. I had a toddler, Selina, two years old, and a baby in my tummy. I knew absolutely nothing of gardening and, frankly, was not that interested. At that time, I was concentrating on looking after my babies, learning about the house and how to cook for large numbers.

The garden was always there, though, and we had the huge benefit of having Roy Balaam as head gardener, who basically took all the decisions about the garden, as I hadn't a clue. It was all a mystery and although we had made a garden at our previous house, it was through the help of a designer, Paul Miles. It was predominantly shrubs and roses, which I learned about by writing their names on labels. It seemed like a new language (although I had loved learning Latin at school).

A whole different ball game greeted me when I arrived at Helmingham in 1975. There were massive borders and strange names like half-hardy annuals, biennials, perennials, corms and bulbs which were all double Dutch to me. But one day I went out into the garden, looked around, and told myself that this was my responsibility, I didn't know what was growing, how it was growing or why, and it came to me that I had better start learning.

Gertrude Jekyll said that the garden is a grand teacher. Luckily, I had a wonderful school in Helmingham, and a brilliant headmaster in Roy, and it is here that I began to understand the right sense of scale and proportion, vital ingredients for a good garden and an invaluable lesson in my design business in later years.

However, it was not until about 1978 that I marched out one day and asked Roy to teach me how to dig. I needed to know from the earth up. He thought (quite wrongly) that I would be better to 'tie up the sweet peas', but I needed to realize what it felt like to dig, and the process that was needed to create and make this important garden sing.

A TOUR OF THE GARDENS

You arrive in the main garden on the west side of the house, along a wide causeway between the house moat and the garden moat. Old yews loll around on the banks and wild flowers are left in serpentine edges of the mown path, wrapping themselves around the topiary.

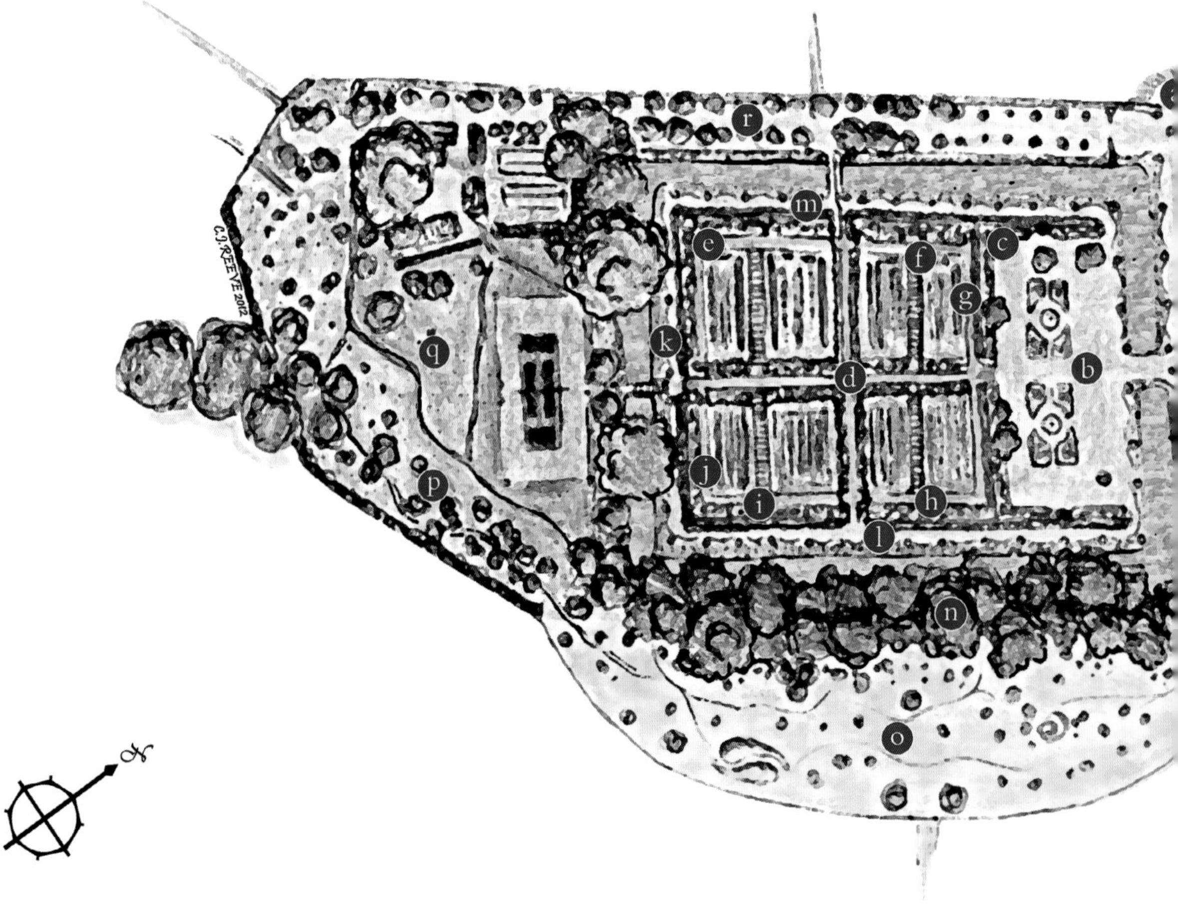

GARDEN PLAN BY CHRIS REEVE

a. Garden Entrance
b. Parterre
c. Hybrid Musk Rose Borders
d. Walled Garden
e. Shrub Border
f. Hot Border
g. Topiary Border
h. Potager
i. Colour- Themed Border
j. Grass Border
k. Late Summer Border
l. Spring Border
m. North Border
n. Yew Walk
o. Woodland Garden
p. Nut Walk
q. Orchard and Wildflower Garden
r. Apple Walk
s. Knot Garden
t. Herb Garden
u. Rose Garden
v. Coach House Lawn
w. Coach House Garden (private)
x. Coach House Tea Rooms
y. Stable Shops

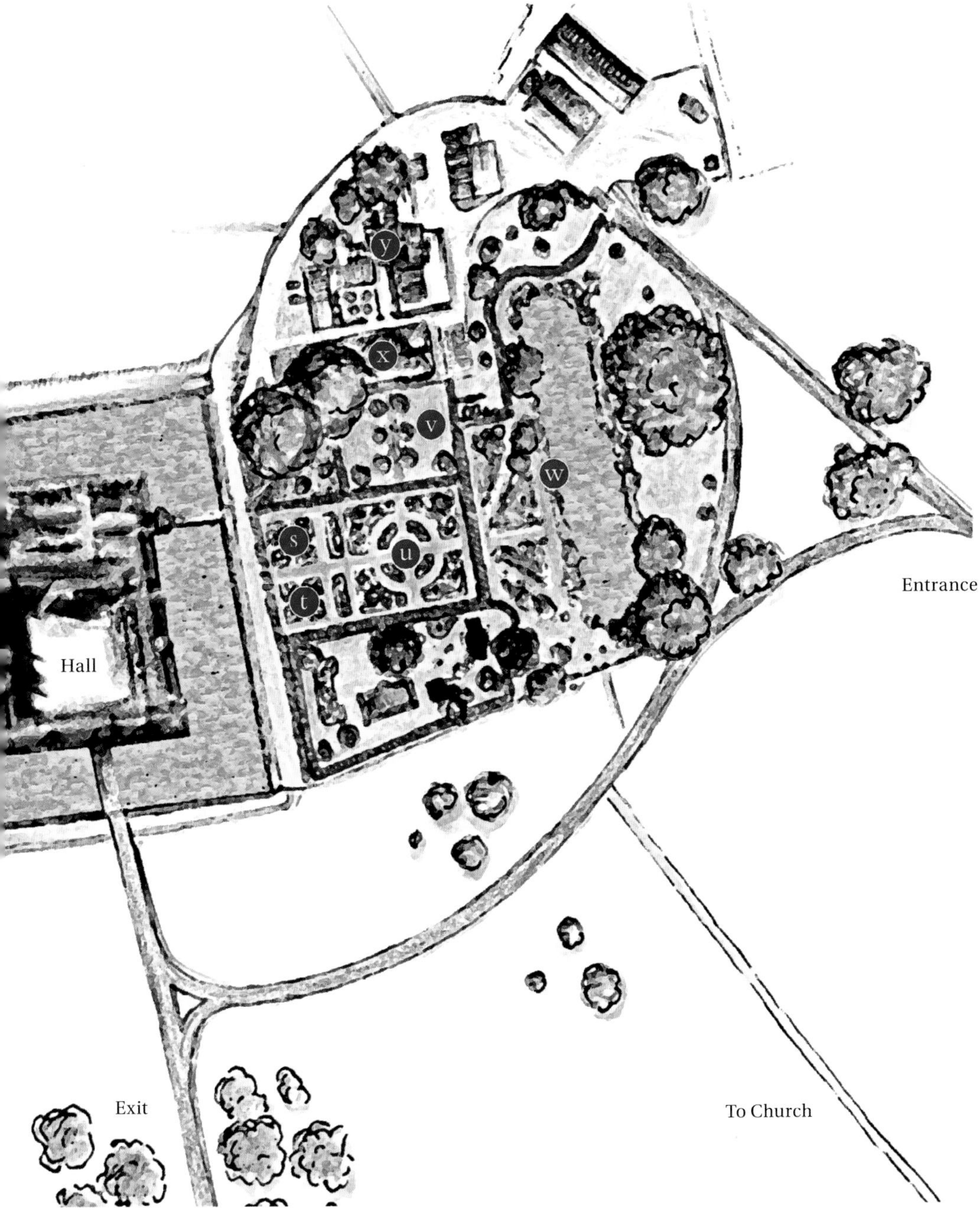

OVERLEAF: My classroom! – an aerial view of the garden

THE PARTERRE

The area where the Parterre is now was in front of Dinah's Hybrid Musk Border and when we took over was planted twice a year with annuals. In the winter there was a lot of brown earth and nothing to see. I wanted to make this a garden to look down on from the upstairs bedrooms, looking good throughout the year, especially in the winter months. But I had to be careful not to dominate the fabulous rose garden which surrounded it. On the contrary, it must complement it.

I had noted the brick obelisks which surround the house and, using these features as a starting point, I planted box obelisks in the centre, edged the beds in box, and filled the space in between with *Santolina chamaecyparissus* (I call it cotton lavender). Alongside its lovely grey foliage, this plant has horrid little yellow flowers: if you cut the plant down in early spring it doesn't flower, which saves you having to cut them off.

BELOW: The Saxon garden moat
BOTTOM: The Parterre and the Hybrid Musk Border
OPPOSITE, ABOVE AND BELOW: The Parterre, with box obelisks underplanted with cotton lavender (*Santolina chamaecyparissus*)

THE HYBRID MUSK BORDER

This is planted on the west side of the house between the moat and the Walled Garden.

My mother-in-law planted it in 1963 to replace old labour-intensive herbaceous borders, and the roses run on three sides of the wall surrounding the Parterre. Having added 'Thisbe', 'Danaë', 'Francesca', 'Nur Mahal', 'Trier' and several climbing roses, I now have almost a complete collection.

Many of the original roses still flower and 'Hidcote' lavender still edges the beds. When people ask me how to keep lavender I point them to this planting and explain that it isn't the fault of the plant if it dies out, it's how it's been treated – or not. It needs to be trimmed every year down to just a little bit of the previous year's growth. This border is a good example of how to grow lavender and keep it looking brilliant after more than fifty years. The repeat planting is magnificent in its simplicity.

I have learned that if a garden works then there is no need to change a winning formula. This area of the garden works, with the bold charismatic border of roses with their underplanting and next to it the simple architectural parterre of green and silver planting. In the centre of the parterre are two magnificent urns on pedestals which are planted twice a year with tulips followed by pelargoniums.

There was a bit of a revelation one day when I went out with Roy to talk about this border that my mother-

in-law had planted. It is breathtakingly beautiful, with large repeat plantings of 'Felicia', 'Cornelia', 'Vanity', 'Daybreak', 'Moonlight', 'Buff Beauty', 'Penelope' and roses in other pastel shades, underplanted with London pride (*Saxifraga* x *urbium*) and *Campanula lactiflora* and edged in 'Hidcote' lavender. However, at some point, for some inexplicable reason, my parents-in-law, John and Dinah, fell for a big blowsy modern orange rose at the Suffolk Show and planted a whole row of it at the front. To my eye this was completely wrong: although I now love orange in my gardens, I couldn't stand it at that time and especially looking at something so modern in this setting of lovely old roses. I mentioned this to Roy, who turned to me and said, 'Well, it's your garden now, if you don't like them, take them out!' Shock, horror, and what would my mother-in-law say? But take them out I did and from that moment I was more confident in making additions and changes to the garden. My mother-in-law was very tactful and never drew attention to her missing roses. I bless her for it. A valuable lesson to be learned.

Around the urns we do annual planting of wallflowers and tulips for the early display and cosmos for the summer show. Two magnificent urns in the centre are seasonally planted to complement the planting below them.

OPPOSITE: Roses 'Felicia', 'Buff Beauty' and 'Cornelia', with *Campanula lactiflora*, in the Hybrid Musk Border
BELOW: The Hybrid Musk Border, with its edging of 'Hidcote' lavender

THE WALLED GARDEN

As you leave this area you go into the Walled Garden, through decorative iron gates with big brick pillars on either side, on top of which are cast-iron heads of Pegasus. Before you there are long double cruciform herbaceous borders, backed by rusty iron posts supporting wirework, along which are trained roses, clematis, honeysuckle and *Lathyrus grandiflorus* (the perennial pea), separating you from the large vegetable plots behind.

By the early 1980s I was becoming familiar with the herbaceous borders, and constantly changing the planting combinations. Over the years I have learned to love plants that previously I had not liked at all. Take dahlias for instance. They were grown traditionally in a row, supported with hazel stakes, because Roy had always done them like that. Good for cutting, and there were some which were unavailable, so, for the sake of history and keeping the plant going, I let them be. Now, I adore them. I not only keep up the rows, I have bought a lot more dahlias each year and trial them in a separate bed before introducing them into the borders, where they flower consistently until the first hard frosts. They do a great job in decorating the church, the house and for pots round the pool house and coach house too.

In the 1980s Tim had discovered old plans which showed that originally the Walled Garden was divided into eight, with more herbaceous borders. Four large and long borders are enough for anyone, I thought, so we made tunnels through the vegetable plots, two to start with, and we made them from bamboo to see if we liked the idea. We planted runner beans up them and as they grew the bamboos got lower and lower, weighed down by the beans. You had to be a small child to walk through them. Any adult had to crawl. Anyway, it gave us confidence to get the tunnels made up in rusty iron sourced locally and Billy, who had worked for us for many years, welded them together. We had successfully divided the borders and taken away the heavy and vast vegetable patches, making eight smaller areas.

The Main Border at midsummer

LEFT: Tunnel of runner bean 'Painted Lady', terminating in a seat by George Carter
BELOW LEFT: The gourd tunnel in all its glory
BELOW RIGHT: Sweet pea tunnel

So what to plant up the tunnels? Runner beans were the obvious choice and so we have 'Scarlet Emperor' runners on one and then 'White Lady' and 'Painted Lady' up the other one. This left two to think about. My first thought was sweet peas and then Tim had the brilliant idea of planting the gourds, which are now a famous hallmark of the Walled Garden.

I now looked at the reduced vegetable patches and thought I was being very boring with the veg. I had visited Rosemary Verey's garden at Barnsley, had admired her potager so much and came back convinced I should do the same. Then I realized that one of my patches was the size of her whole potager – and I had eight! It would drive Roy crazy too, with having to plant and pick in shapes. I began to appreciate the horticultural excellence of his vegetables and how beautiful a row of perfect onions looks, and rows of dead-straight broad beans. So I forgot that idea . . . (However, I did make a potager later.)

I always make notes every three weeks or so, to remember what is looking good or what hasn't worked. It is so difficult to remember when the whole lot has been cut down. Some of my best plant combinations have been accidents and now I re-create them on purpose. Take *Gladiolus* 'The Bride'. Some self-seeded *Nigella damascena* came up through – the combination looked magic. It was photographed by both Jerry and Marcus Harpur. I had to admit it was a happy accident – but sometimes the best things come by force of nature.

In the last generation, there was nothing flowering until late May. Tim remembers his mother and father showing guests round the garden and there was nothing out, save one peony. This was because there were then many more annuals in the beds, which of course didn't flower till June or July. There were large corners of annuals planted at each crossing of paths and at the ends of the borders. That was one of the first things I reorganized, planting with perennials instead.

ABOVE: *Dahlia* 'Twyning's After Eight'

Now we have early daffodils, tulips and alliums all flowering from March onwards. The borders are almost completely filled with perennials, flowering until the asters finish off in November. In the early part of the season, the borders are all the soft pastel colours but as the light strengthens the colours get hotter and the bronzes, reds and yellows come to the fore. We lengthen the flowering season with a few annuals and dahlias planted where early perennials have died down. For instance, the large Oriental poppies like 'Mrs Perry' die a very ungraceful death, leaving huge ugly brown leaves and a large open space. So, we cut them down and plant annuals like *Tagetes patula* or dahlias which we have potted up in anticipation. We also plant cosmos, antirrhinums, ammi and tobacco plants to fill any gaps. By the end of July we have the borders billowing out with an exuberance that continues well after we close with our Plant Heritage Fair at the end of September.

By 1990 my consuming passion was for plants, and the idea of adding to the variety of plants with shrubs and grasses (which were not in evidence at Helmingham before) made me start thinking more about the Walled Garden. The simple fact was that we were growing far too many vegetables and too much fruit. Both were time-consuming and expensive – and I could not sell, eat, freeze, bottle, preserve or make alcoholic drinks from all the produce. (Mulberry vodka is terrific, but cabbage gin does not have the same appeal, somehow.)

In the Walled Garden, at the base of the high walls, were big, deep borders – 2–3 metres/7–10 feet deep in places. This opportunity was too tempting for me to resist, so I started making use of all the spare bits and bobs that people had given me and that I didn't know where to plant. The first border at the top of the Main Border was east-facing, quite damp and shady, with no full purpose. I was not taking away anything of use or beauty, so I felt quite free to plant it with unusual shrubs underplanted with ferns and a few perennials. This had the almost immediate effect of giving an anchor to the garden (as well as eventually completely covering it with plants, thereby reducing the need for endless weeding).

Once the tunnels were planted up it was obvious that they should finish at each end with a focal point. I asked my great friend George Carter to make me two benches, which I surrounded by big box hedges, with a York stone square as a sitting area. At the opposite ends were two urns on pedestals with a curved yew hedge as a backdrop. Having done this, it was even more obvious that these focal points needed planting either side, so every year we created a new border, replacing either vegetables or rows of fruit. We now have eight of these big, deep borders all planted with a different theme.

OPPOSITE: The Main Border in late summer

THE COLOUR-THEMED BORDER

My Colour-Themed Border is separated by thick yew buttresses. The border faces north, so doesn't get the sun until midday. It is extraordinary how quickly yew trees actually grow, and they are a big benefit to the garden, giving it structure. In between the buttresses are perennials, and here I experiment with colour combinations. This brings out the artist in me and I so enjoy seeing what colours go well together. We were careful to put a root guard down the sides of the yew hedge, as otherwise the roots would take all the goodness out of the soil, causing the perennials to suffer and die back. This border is designed to look at its best when the main borders are having a bit of a rest.

The top section has pink and red plants, the second section has red and purple, the next one shows off purple and blue flowers, then we go to the yellows and oranges for the last two sections.

BELOW: The reds in the Colour-Themed Border, including *Gladiolus* 'Ruby'
RIGHT: *Agapanthus* 'Jack's Blue' and *Miscanthus sinensis* 'Flamingo' in the blue section

THE GRASS BORDER

Adjacent to the Colour-Themed Border, facing east, is my border of grasses. For a long time I failed to see the beauty and use of these ornamental grasses. I couldn't see why people got so keen on something that didn't flower, as I understood it. Now I love them for their movement and grace, as well as for their value to the winter garden and to wildlife.

I have planted big, bold drifts of grasses with unusual shrubs including *Heptacodium miconoides, Lonicera involucrata* and *Euphorbia mellifera.* Here I have hellebores and pulmonarias that flower in the late winter and spring, spiked by white hyacinths. We cut down the old leaves of the hellebores by Christmas so that when the beautiful flowers appear they are not hidden by scraggly old growth. (I cut them for the house but, as with poppies, the stems need to be seared in boiling water before you put them in a vase.)

Grasses seem like a modern trend, but looking back in old catalogues, they were well used in Victorian gardens.

BELOW LEFT: *Calamagrostis brachytricha*
BELOW RIGHT: *Kniphofia* 'Jenny Bloom'

THE POTAGER

Now I have a potager! This is on the north-facing wall, next to the Colour-Themed Border. I had buttresses made up echoing the shape of the yew buttresses in that border, but in wirework. We then installed these wirework buttresses in the Potager to create compartments for (mainly) edible plants, which

were planted in a consciously designed way, paying attention to combinations of colour and shape. Here are perennial horseradish, rhubarb, artichokes, parsnips and onions (both of which are left to flower), *Cerinthe major* 'Purpurascens', beetroot 'Bull's Blood', *Crambe maritima*, thyme, basil, chives, parsley and the asparagus pea, also known as poor man's asparagus. This has enchanting small pea-like red flowers, and I also plant it at the feet of the young gourd plants, to give interest there in the early stages. (But I would have to be fairly desperate to pick it for lunch, as it's quite bitter.) An interesting plant is *Sedum reflexum*, a very old stonecrop (also known as Trip-Madame and Prick-Madame). The wirework buttresses also allow us to grow climbing plants, including *Ipomoea tricolor* 'Heavenly Blue', sweet peas and climbing sunflowers. We try new annual varieties each year, to give a different look to both the Potager and our salad bowls.

ABOVE: *Ipomoea tricolor* 'Heavenly Blue' in the Potager
BELOW: The Topiary Border, featuring 'Jekka' thyme – and Maestro

THE TOPIARY BORDER

Another long, slim border runs the entire width of the Walled Garden. This has given us a lot of fun. South-facing, it was formerly known as the Peach Border, as we had (and still have) peaches and nectarines growing here. (We have tried various varieties of peach and find the white-skinned 'Peregrine' is the best, with 'Amsden June' also a reliable variety.)

After my Theatrical Garden at the Chelsea Flower Show in 2001, I was left with a lot of good-sized plants of box and yew. No one was going to buy these and I could not bear to see them go in the skip. I brought them home and stuck them in this bed and I told them to let me know what they wanted to be. Did they want to be a cloud, or an egg, or a doughnut?

Nowadays at the end of the show all the gardens at Chelsea are moved elsewhere, so saving the plants, which can go on to give pleasure in such places as hospices and care homes.

Box topiary 'The Frog Prince' and 'Miss Jekyll's Working Boot' in the Topiary Border

I also brought home some nearly black *Iris* 'Sable' from this show and they went in as well, to give contrast in foliage. For a different flowering time I planted white lavender – thus creating a reduced and simple planting palette.

The shapes soon let us know what they were destined to be and Chris Reeve has expertly clipped them into their forms. We have acorns, a snail, a bee and a garden boot (which has turned, more elaborately, into Miss Jekyll's famous working boot). A snowman has appeared and a couple of rabbits and a frog with a crown on his head. Humour is definitely allowed in the garden!

Also allowed to thrive are delphiniums, which always struggled in the densely planted herbaceous borders. Here they have room to show off and, with deadheading and cutting down, amazingly they have a second flowering.

'Sammy Snail' and other topiary creations, among mixed delphiniums grown from seed

THE HOT BORDER

And, what is more, we now have a Hot Border. This is at right angles to the Topiary Border. For years I loathed anything orange in the garden. Now, I can't get enough of it. (Isn't this interesting?) This border has purple-foliage plants such as *Berberis thunbergii* 'Helmond Pillar' and purple-leaved cannas. Red-hot sizzling colours are provided mainly by annuals and dahlias, so of course it is on fire at the end of the summer. I adore it. It faces south and so gets a lot of sun. *Dahlia* 'David Howard', *D.* 'Bishop of Llandaff' and *Alstroemeria* Indian Summer are substantial plants that create fireworks.

Against the wall here in this south-facing border we have the advantage of a beautifully trained fig tree. 'Brown Turkey' is the variety.

My favourite rose, Munstead Wood, is in the Hot Border, and although it isn't 'hot' it looks so good with

OPPOSITE: *Dahlia* 'Princess Royal' in front of a seat designed by George Carter, with the Hot Border beyond
ABOVE LEFT: *Eschscholzia californica* (California poppy)
ABOVE TOP RIGHT: *Canna* 'Orange Glow'
ABOVE BOTTOM RIGHT: *Dahlia* 'Faith' and an unidentified dark red dahlia

the other reds and oranges that it is allowed to stay. We sow the annual marigold *Tagetes patula*, a taller-growing variety given to me by Ivan Dickings, a superb plantsman who was so generous to me over the years. Cannas are planted annually and *Ipomoea lobata* is trained up some obelisks.

Other borders under the walls house shrubs, perennials and roses, the different aspects of the garden growing the appropriate fruit: apples and pears, plums, greengages and peaches, figs and nectarines all grow against the walls.

As you leave the Walled Garden you can visit three different long borders, all within the moat and wrapping themselves round the walls on three sides.

CLOCKWISE FROM TOP LEFT: *Paeonia* 'Buckeye Belle'; *P. lactiflora* 'Baroness Schröder'; *P.l.* 'Sarah Bernhardt' (with rose 'Goldfinch'); *P.l.* 'Krinkled White'
OPPOSITE: The Spring Border with ox-eye daisies flowing in and out
OVERLEAF: The Spring Border, with valerian among the peonies and the climbing roses (including, in the foreground, deep pink 'Sophie's Perpetual')

THE SPRING BORDER

One is the Spring Border. The tulips come first, a sweetie box of colours, preceded by 'Apeldoorn', a wonderful red tulip which, unlike modern tulips, actually multiplies. It has been there for over sixty years. I soon found that when I chose lovely tulips at the Chelsea Flower Show and planted them in groups of fifteen, they were fabulous the first year, the second produced maybe nine and by the third year there would be a measly three – or, worse, two! Meanwhile my attention would be taken by another kind and I would plant them in groups once again. The following year a yellow tulip would appear among my lovely new pink ones – I may have been converted to orange, but I still cannot reconcile myself to the combination of yellow and pink.

I have learned from my mistakes and now for my clients I plant colours that will seamlessly combine and look good together: as long as the colours are sympathetic, it doesn't matter where they pop up.

The border then produces irises and, lastly, peonies. These great plants are fantastic and I cannot help myself ordering just one more tree peony or a herbaceous peony. They are magic for nearly three months and then they're over – and it's tough for visitors who don't see the peonies at their glorious best – but then something else takes precedence and is shouting, 'look at me now!' *Paeonia* 'Buckeye Belle', *P. lactiflora* 'White Wings' and *P.l.* 'Bowl of Beauty' are among my favourites and the staggering tree peony *P. rockii* can have thirty blooms on it at one time. (This plant too was given to me by Ivan Dickings.)

Old roses cover the walls, but they have been joined by some that I brought back from my Chelsea gardens and one new firm favourite called Open Arms. It looks wonderful against the brick walls and flowers prolifically with small delicate pink single flowers. It also has the advantage of very glossy healthy foliage.

THE NORTH BORDER

On the north side is a narrow border where I have practised my philosophy on tulips. I have black and white varieties and it doesn't matter if they are Cottage, Darwin hybrid, Parrot or Lily-flowered: this colour combination always works.

Amazingly, the *Campanula lactiflora* from over the wall did a gigantic leap of faith and seeded itself here. We do the 'Chelsea chop' with these plants, cutting half of them down in Chelsea week to about 75 cm/30 inches high, which means that they flower later. Spring bulbs line this border.

THE LATE SUMMER BORDER

On the west side is the Late Summer Border, which is a silver, pink and white border with shrubs, especially hydrangeas, which do well in this shady and damp side of the garden, helped by the shade of an ancient oak tree leaning over the garden moat. Here the lovely *Deutzia setchuenensis* var. *corymbiflora* flowers, as well as various viburnums. More climbing roses and clematis scramble through the shrubs and up the walls.

BEYOND THE GARDEN MOAT

In October 1987, there was the disastrous hurricane which devastated great swathes of southern England, including the Helmingham estate. Tim was at home and I was in London and he told me he woke up in the night to feel the house shaking. Looking out the next morning was like a horror movie. I think that over the estate we lost four hundred trees. The wonderful Oak Avenue, planted in 1680, was desecrated, with a great number of trees down. Among the other losses were two ancient mulberry trees by the Parterre. This was an especially heavy blow as we had a letter in the library, dated 1623, asking the gardeners to 'look after my new Mulberry trees'. The huge job of clearing up took most of the following winter. The next spring, we were amazed to find the mulberries had tiny little signs of new growth. Since then, they have grown into significantly fine trees again.

OPPOSITE: The garden moat in spring
ABOVE: Young trees in the Oak Avenue

THE APPLE WALK

Amazingly, the storm brought some pluses too. The two cedars at the end of the Apple Walk were very dramatic, but they died after the hurricane and we had to fell them. Riding out in the park one day, I was astonished to have a fine view of the house that I had never seen before. So we did not replant: instead, we continued the Apple Walk with new apple trees, based on old Suffolk and Norfolk seedlings.

Later, our new head gardener, Brendan Arundel, who started in the garden in March 2021, suggested we should stop mowing behind the row of trees and allow the wild flowers to grow. This proved to be highly successful, with buttercups and cowslips in abundance, followed by ox-eye daisies and large numbers of orchids. Recently we had the great excitement of the appearance of pyramidal orchids (*Anacamptis pyramidalis*), including two magnificent and rare white ones (*A.p.* var. *albiflora*). We hope they will multiply. (To think we had been mowing them for years!)

This simple fruit-lined walk within the curtilage of the garden and overlooking the park taught me a valuable lesson: that after the hectic planting of the Walled Garden, there was a need for 'nothing' to rest the soul and mind and be able to look over the magnificent park with its old oak trees. Now in my plans for clients I always try to find such a space for 'nothing'.

CLOCKWISE FROM RIGHT: Apple blossom in spring; George Carter's seat at the end of the Apple Walk; apples in autumn

THE WILDFLOWER GARDEN

The Wildflower Garden is a magical area beyond the tennis court and on the outskirts of the park fence. People are always asking how to create something as beautiful as this. The answer is that it has always been there; it's just the correct treatment every year that retains its beauty. Yellow rattle feeds off the grass, clearing space for the wild flowers. There is a carpet of yellow primroses and cowslips followed by ox-eye daisies and camassias; then orchids and wild grasses appear, along with the other late-flowering species. We cut it down in August, leave it for ten days to allow the flower seeds to drop and then rake it off by hand (a hard job). We might give it another cut before Christmas. Old fruit trees, apples and quinces line this meadow, and a hazel hedge is now sufficiently established for it to be coppiced for the hazel supports we need for the borders.

RIGHT, ABOVE:
The bee orchid,
Ophrys apifera
RIGHT, BELOW:
The pyramidal orchid,
Anacamptis pyramidalis
BELOW: Ox-eye daisies
in the Wildflower Garden

THE WOODLAND GARDEN

I dreamed of making another garden to celebrate the new millennium, but it was necessary first to dredge the garden moat. A complicated procedure was carried out, ending with the moat looking wonderful, clear of weed and much more significant – so it was a good idea after all. (Unfortunately, no gold cirques were found, only a bit of blue and white pottery.)

I had been thinking of creating a Woodland Garden for some time. On the south-west side of the Walled Garden is a thick yew walk. My mother-in-law tried to plant under it and I similarly tried, but yews are greedy and take all the moisture, and so the soil is undernourished and always dry. There is now a good ground covering and a few shade-tolerant shrubs do pretty well, but it is impossible to grow anything interesting. However, we definitely need protection from the prevailing winds and the ancient tall yews provide this vital shelter for the garden.

We limbed up the old yews, removing all the lower branches, and the evening light now shines through them. However, there was still a hard straight line and the shrubs were pruned greedily by hungry deer. We thought we would take out the iron park railings that were tight to these yew trees and move them some distance away into the park. (I judged that it would be good to replicate the curve of the drive as it went away from the front of the house.) Moving the fence out allowed the many shrubs that Dinah had planted to re-establish and billow out. There, lovely arbutus, several berberis, philadelphus, lots of lilac and laburnum finally had the freedom to grow.

Moreover, when we moved the railings out to form the new Woodland Garden, it was very exciting to start planning the trees that we would plant. It was lovely to think that I now had space to plant the type of trees that would not look right in a Tudor deer park alongside English oaks. I could choose the more domestic trees – crab apples, cherries, birches, sorbus, acers and several conifers. I have zelkova and sophora, cryptomeria, aesculus and liquidambar among the bigger trees, and I bought from Neil Lucas three elms propagated from *Ulmus americana* 'Princeton', which is reckoned to be resistant to Dutch elm disease. Fifteen years on, two are still looking good (one of them died, but of other causes).

I thought that doing this would be a worthwhile investment. My line of thinking to justify the costs was that it might be impossible for future generations to keep up a very expensive and labour-intensive walled garden and so therefore there should be a low-maintenance established garden for them to enjoy. I wanted a loose design to it.

I vowed not to overplant, however tempting (a mistake I had made too many times in the past). I planted the larger trees further away from the yew walk and the smaller trees and shrubs nearer to it, so there was a natural progression towards the larger landscape of the park.

I had learned from the Apple Walk that it is important to have a stretch of green simplicity before the park starts and I follow that rule in my designs. It is tempting to try to put too much into the design (to give the client their money's worth), but it is vital to allow the sense of space and something to rest the eyes on after the exuberant planting elsewhere.

Anyway, I realized that once the trees had established there would be heavy canopies and that it would be quite a shady garden. To give light I planted a circle of crab apples and one of cherries, both smaller trees that would allow a mown grassy glade in their centre. The first trees to go in were three *Betula utilis* subsp. *jacquemontii* which I had bought for Ed and Sophie's wedding and had in the church hall.

It still lacked something – it looked flat. And so I decided to have some land sculpture, not on the scale of Charles Jencks or Kim Wilkie, but mini-landforms. I loved the idea of a grass mound but wanted something to make it more interesting.

I was meanwhile working on a garden in the United States (in Virginia), and at that time was designing a wood. It was hard work and on the last day I was running up and down a slippery steep hill desperately placing and planting the last of 250 trees before I had to leave to catch the flight home. Something had to give and the cartilage on my knee was the victim. I was told to rest it.

Having so admired and been so jealous of Jerry's skill on his digger – he had been hired to create my first Chelsea garden – I had taken a digger-driving course of my own. It seemed to me this was the perfect way of resting my knee and so I hired a digger and set about doing the landform, which I had decided was to be a yin-yang design. It was hilarious trying to do it without any experience and Roy was frequently brought in with cries for help. Finally, it was finished and the turf pegged down. My smart green serpents were born!

Needless to say, the digger bug had got to me and a few years later I did a downward turf spiral in the same garden. This was much more complicated. I hired the digger again for a very expensive week, so I was on that digger from 9 a.m. to 5 p.m., which fried my brain. I was absolutely exhausted at the end of it. (I was told later that driving a digger makes much the same demands on your brain as flying a helicopter!) Again, I crawled to my garden team and we did the last bit by hand. The spiral has a pool at the bottom and children love paddling in it, with newts for company. A few years later I thought it would be good to have a middle layer of planting, so I added to the yin-yang mounds three intertwining teardrop beds planted with grasses and *Oenothera* (syn. *Gaura*) *lindheimeri*. This planting looks interesting and beautiful all season long.

The Woodland Garden is now well established and it again provides a viewing platform for the park, just as the Apple Walk does on the other side.

ABOVE: The Woodland Garden
BELOW: The yin-yang mounds, Maestro in attendance

THE KNOT AND HERB GARDENS

In the 1950s and 1960s, my father-in-law was very keen on ornamental wildfowl and so, on the east side of the house, he had created a home for a large collection of rare birds. They were encased by a high wire fence and had little concrete bird baths, a few species roses and a fine cherry tree. They were exactly in front of the house and on the side where we live most of the time.

Added to that, we had put in a swimming pool soon after we moved in, as by then we had two small children and I wanted to teach them to swim as early as possible. (Bringing up children surrounded by a wide moat with a parapet and a steep drop is not the most relaxing pastime.) The pool was on the south side of the wildfowl area. Therefore, in order to reach it, the children would run through all the duck poo to get there. Then too, one of my pet hates is keeping birds with clipped wings. Birds should fly if they were born to do so and therefore it was fairly pleasing when my small but energetic Jack Russell terrier managed to capture and dispose of them all, one by one.

BELOW AND ON PAGE 59: Lady Salisbury's watercolours of the Knot and Herb Gardens

This gave us the freedom to make a completely new garden, putting our own stamp on the place – but what to do and where to go?

I took myself off on a solo garden tour, visiting many counties where there were houses of similar age to Helmingham and studying what had been done with historical sensitivity. I had a wonderful time, ending each day in a small town or village and finding a suitable (or in some cases highly unsuitable) bed and breakfast wherever I ended up.

This was long before my design business started and I did not know how to design this new garden layout myself. All I did know was that it should be a symmetrical garden meant to look down upon from the wide raised bed and also from the windows of the house. A meandering garden (which I yearned for) was not for here. So I asked the late Marchioness of Salisbury if she could advise me. The Old Palace at Hatfield is the same age as Helmingham. She informed me that she was now designing gardens professionally, and agreed to come over to talk about it.

She arrived, and we went out and discussed how and from where we should reach the garden, and how we could incorporate it with the swimming pool area and the

Coach House opposite (this is a beautiful classical building that had been turned into the tea room for open days).

She told me that it was very important, historically, to have a knot garden. Meekly I agreed, and added that I had thought of using the fret that is part of the family crest. But I also wanted a herb garden, and a home for the collection of old-fashioned roses that I had started after seeing Humphrey Brooke's amazing rose garden nearby. Mollie Salisbury made the whole of my wish list come true. She drew up a design with two box knot gardens, each divided into four squares. All four squares of one garden were to be planted with herbs, and the other was to have the family fret in two squares and our initials in the other two. (T and A: believe it or not, my name is Alexandra, but of course no one calls me that, as I have been Xa all my life.) The Knot Garden is planted mainly with genera introduced in Britain before 1750 (with a few more modern hybrids secretly slipped in), while the Herb Garden is planted with short-growing perennial herbs. Two rectangular rose beds follow on, and then there is the main Rose Garden.

ABOVE, BELOW AND OPPOSITE: The Herb and Knot Gardens

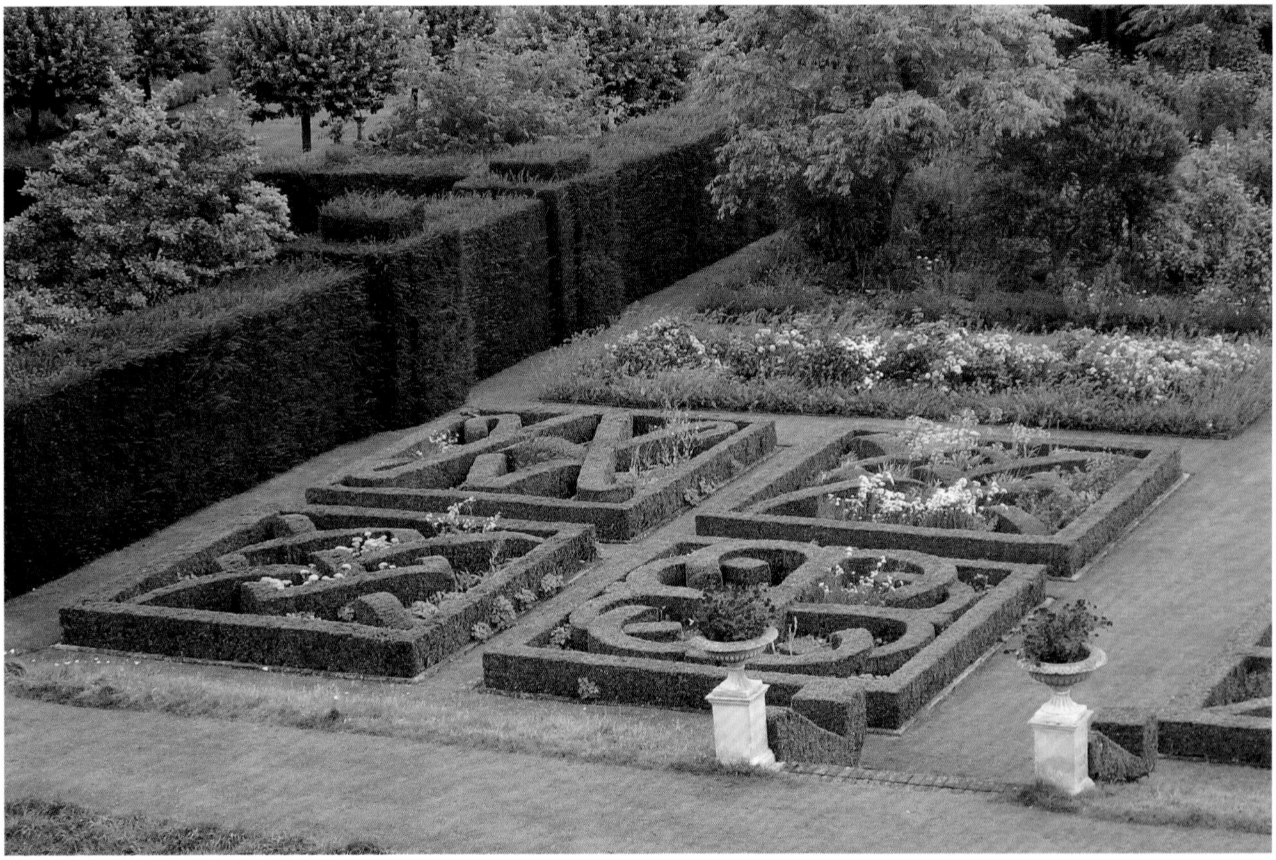

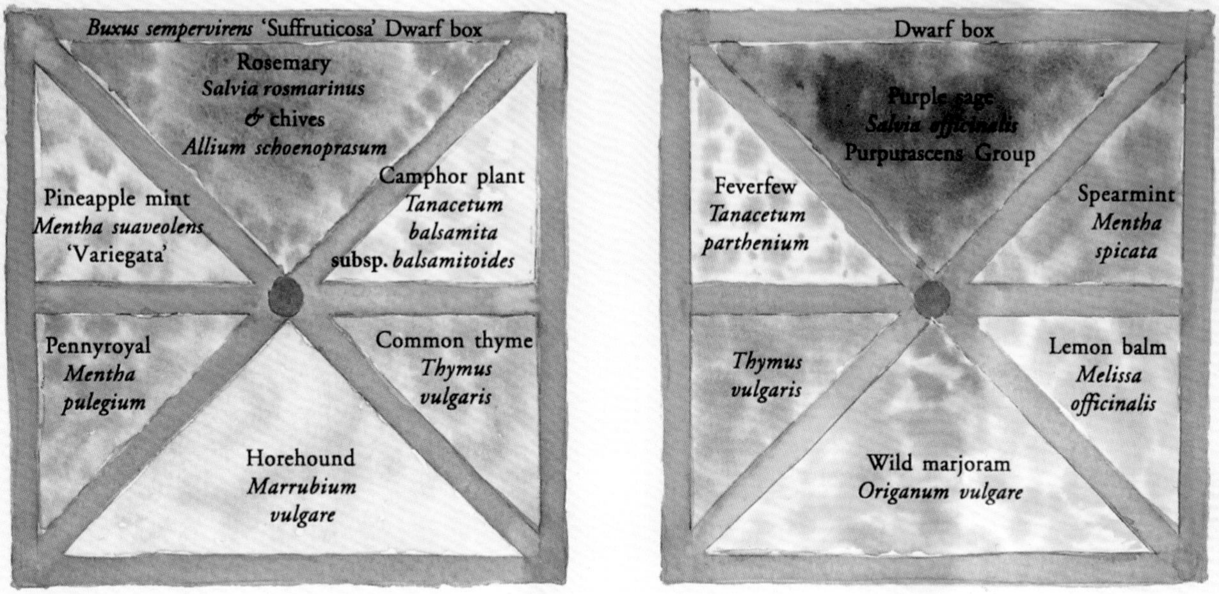
Buxus sempervirens 'Suffruticosa' Dwarf box
Rosemary
Salvia rosmarinus
& chives
Allium schoenoprasum
Pineapple mint
Mentha suaveolens
'Variegata'
Camphor plant
Tanacetum
balsamita
subsp. *balsamitoides*
Pennyroyal
Mentha
pulegium
Common thyme
Thymus
vulgaris
Horehound
Marrubium
vulgare
Dwarf box
Purple sage
Salvia officinalis
Purpurascens Group
Feverfew
Tanacetum
parthenium
Spearmint
Mentha
spicata
Thymus
vulgaris
Lemon balm
Melissa
officinalis
Wild marjoram
Origanum vulgare

THE ROSE GARDEN

Beyond the Knot Garden is the Rose Garden. Marking the division are two rectangular beds planted with Rosa Mundi (*Rosa gallica* 'Versicolor'), *R.* 'The Fairy' and *R.* 'White Pet'.

I don't like roses with bare legs and so we have planted forget-me-nots and bergenia to provide the cover. This means that the beds flower continuously from March to November.

These beds lead to the main Rose Garden, comprising four quadrant beds, each of them growing varieties of roses of similar types or dates. We have species and Alba roses in one bed, Centifolia and Moss roses in another, Bourbons, Gallicas and Damask roses growing together in the third bed and Rugosas, China roses and Hybrid Perpetuals in the fourth. These are all underplanted with foxgloves, geraniums and some later-flowering perennials.

In the middle is a bed of golden thyme: here stands a statue of Flora holding her garland of roses. The thyme bed is surrounded by four semicircular beds planted with David Austin's new English roses We feed these every six weeks so that they repeat-flower to the end of the season.

The paths are mown grass and all the beds are edged with soldier-laid bricks, giving a very crisp look (and the beds need less edging, too).

The whole of the Rose Garden is encased by a high yew hedge, for which various people have given me advice. Roy Strong came one day and said it was very boring having just a straight hedge and that I should topiarize it. I didn't do exactly what he suggested but I took the point and we now have buttresses and different heights. I was puzzled by how to get to the end of this garden and into the next, a much more informal woodland area. Emma Tennant came up with the suggestion that we

OPPOSITE: Rosa Mundi, with an edging of 'Walker's Low' catmint
LEFT, ABOVE: *Rosa* 'Desdemona'
LEFT, BELOW: Rosa Mundi
BELOW: *Rosa* 'Princess Alexandra of Kent'

shouldn't make an entrance/exit at all, but instead just cut out a window. Access should be round in two other ways. Genius, I thought.

About five years after planting this garden, I went out one lovely sunny evening and saw all my new roses doing so well and, thinking that all the colours blended beautifully, felt quite proud. It poured with rain all that night and I went out next morning to find all the roses lying flat, the flowers blown off and petals scattering the ground. My instant tears turned to rage and then a vow to do something to eradicate this destruction.

Having researched the tying down practised in the Victorian age, I designed the Helmingham Rose Support, which consists of a dome-shaped metal frame to which the rose can be tied. (See the drawing on page 169.) The result is that the plant flowers all the way down its stem and the new growth comes up and flops over the tied-down branches, thus forming an informal shrub which resembles full crinoline skirts of pinks, whites and reds. The Supports have now been in our Rose Garden for years, and the roses are tied down in this way every February.

Apparently, I was cleverer than I thought and this action of tying down sends the enzymes to the end of the stem. They catch the light, and flowers are produced all the way down. Dr Dave Hessayon of *The Garden Expert* fame told me this.

Being a designer, I am conscious of giving credit to people who have contributed. There have been a few clients in my career who have never acknowledged that I designed their garden and seem almost ashamed that they needed help. I used to be sensitive to that and felt hurt on a few occasions, but I guess it is just part of human frailty.

So I always tell people that Lady Salisbury designed the Rose Garden. I did the planting plan (mainly because I felt that if I made mistakes, it was not going to cost too much). However, I was constantly ringing up to ask her advice.

Rosa 'Marchesa Boccella' (syn. 'Jacques Cartier') and *R.* 'Ispahan', both grown on Helmingham Rose Supports

THE COACH HOUSE GARDEN

Following on in an easterly direction from the Rose Garden is a magical area which includes the rectangular pond where they would water the horses that were stabled in the Coach House. This is an elliptical stretch of water with big weeping willows. We decided to take the deer fence away from the far edge and put it on the edge of the drive, thereby creating more space behind the pond where we have planted several interesting species of oaks. The cork oak, *Quercus suber*, is really quite large now. (It was given to me, as were so many of the plants in the garden, by Jamie Chichester, whose famous nursery, Chichester Trees and Shrubs, I use constantly in my design business. They are usually able to produce everything on my wish list.)

I wanted also to plant trees that gave us some height and colour (and, again, trees that would not have looked right in the park). Underneath these trees we planted long grass and wild flowers which have naturalized wonderfully.

I planted up the Horse Drinking Pond with a mixture of water-loving plants and grasses and, on the other side, gunnera, bamboo, grasses and a collection of willows.

When I had just arrived to live at Helmingham, many kind and intensely knowledgeable gardeners such as Humphrey Brooke, John Blakenham and Maxwell Eley would invite us (the young!) over to look at their gardens and they would say to me, 'Do you see all this?' (waving their arms to show the vast trees around us), 'I planted all these.' I would think that this was an incredible feat – and also that these knowledgeable horticulturists must be very, very old. However, the other day I was walking through my mini-arboretum and suddenly I looked round, 'Crikey, I planted all this!' It is now almost forty years old. Of course, I planted some things far too close and have had to remove some of the thugs, a lesson I learned to my cost, but it is a haven of informality.

ABOVE LEFT: The Coach House Garden and the Horse Drinking Pond
ABOVE RIGHT: A gate made from the ironwork panels created by John Churchill for my 1997 Chelsea garden (see page 86)

I have learned from wonderful books and *The Education of a Gardener* by Russell Page was especially well read. I learned from him that the garden must curtsy to the house and that formality should be near or around the house, and as you go further into the landscape, the more informal it can be. I always use this as an example in my design business and it always works naturally and seamlessly.

My favourite place in this Coach House Garden is my fire pit. This was actually created in 2004, when I had been riding in Spain with friends and we used to have a fire on the ground and a delicious dinner would be cooked on it. I created one for us by digging a shallow dish and lining it with bricks laid on sand so the water drains through. To edge it we used a tractor wheel. I had a frame made to put a heavy iron tray on and I cook delicious little delicacies on it, or a paella or risotto. A very large oak tree came down and I used some of the wood to make large cubes and small low cubes which I varnished with Danish oil. I produced one for Tim as a Christmas present and I think he thought I had gone potty. However, there is no pain in sitting down on a warm summer night on these large cubes, with a nice bottle and a glass on the small cubes, discussing worldly matters round a roaring fire. I also used to have midnight feasts with my grandchildren: we toasted marshmallows and sang campfire songs and did dervish dancing around the flames.

ABOVE LEFT: Yellow flag iris (*Iris pseudacorus*) on the banks of the Horse Drinking Pond
ABOVE RIGHT: My fire pit, beneath a cherry tree in full blossom

LEAVING

In 2013 we started talking about handing over Helmingham to our son Edward and his wife, Sophie. We had established the fact that they were willing to take up this rather daunting prospect and to move out of London with their children to bring them up in the country at Helmingham. We agreed that 2017 would be a good time for us to leave and for them to move in. This seemed a long way ahead – but, of course, time flies and we soon needed to start organizing it all. We had decided to move back into the lovely old farmhouse where we had started our married life, and that needed a fair amount of work.

Edward and Sophie had both insisted that I should continue looking after the garden, but I had to make a few decisions.

I was dying to create a new garden in my new home, though, of course, it would have to be low-maintenance. I knew, with increasing garden projects all over the country and abroad, I wouldn't be able to give Helmingham the time I had previously. I wasn't going to go out in my pyjamas at 5 or 6 a.m. or garden till dark – not with a comfortable new home nearby and a new garden demanding attention.

I had to reduce the workload so that Roy, who was by then working in the mornings only, and Chris and Graham could manage, with the part-time help of Katherine. It was decided among all of us that the high level of horticulture should not be reduced or compromised.

So, therefore, I took two large rectangular areas of the vegetable plots in the Walled Garden out of productivity – I didn't imagine Sophie wanted or had need of 36,000 Brussels sprouts – and in their stead I designed and produced two new plantings. They had to be low-maintenance and yet different, interesting and – most importantly – beautiful.

The first one has four *Prunus fruticosa* 'Globosa', one in each corner. Down the middle there are three ellipses: two with *P.* 'Amanogawa' (one in each) and 'Hidcote' lavender and the third with the annual *Ageratum houstonianum* 'Blue Horizon' to lengthen the flowering season. In the middle of this bed is a stunning

OPPOSITE: The Pixie Mix spiral, and Pixie Mix in close up
RIGHT: Roy Balaam, Head Gardener at Helmingham for fifty-six years

spiral obelisk sculpture by the artist Pete Moorhouse. This area only requires mowing, the cutting of the lavender and the raising of the easy ageratum.

The area opposite the Elliptical Garden presented a problem. We had to prepare this for sowing grass seed and then leave it to settle. This had happened by April 2016.

I have a weakness for spirals and so I put out lengths of hosepipe to create a spiral border on this newly prepared lawn, easy to manage for the mower to go round and turn in the centre.

It was getting late and we had to think of something to put in this border. Nothing seemed interesting enough, so just for one year I planted a low mix of annual wild flowers from a Pictorial Meadows seed mix. I chose the classic 'Pixie Mix', as the plants grew low and need no staking. The result was so spectacular that we repeat it every year. In the four corners I planted *Prunus* 'Amanogawa' trees for height and to mirror those opposite. Children love running into the waist-high floral mix spiral and out again. It flowers from June to October.

This reduction of labour has meant that our fabulous team is able to keep the garden in tip-top form.

THE GARDENERS

The garden has always been worked hard, from those very early days growing fruit, vegetables and flowers for the house and then later on throughout the war when its produce helped feed all the evacuees. Our present situation is that we have the equivalent of three full-time gardeners, two or three volunteers, and me.

Roy Balaam

Roy Balaam, the long-time Head Gardener, started work here when he was fourteen years old. The story goes thus. Roy was head boy at Helmingham School. My father-in-law saw him and his brother collecting fresh water from the well in the village. The boys stepped back and took their hats off to let the car pass. John was very impressed with this and asked if Roy would like to work in the garden. That is where Roy remained for sixty-five years. He worked under Dan Pilgrim and Charlie Fairweather (a fine name for a gardener) and learned all his trade by experience and by listening to radio gardening programmes. He was made Head Gardener at the age of twenty-three, when Mr Pilgrim and Mr Fairweather retired, and he just had to get on with it.

Roy has now retired, but is a constant support and still lives within the park, in the back lodge. He has gained so much respect, far and wide. I call him the fountain of all knowledge in the gardening world and he has been so supportive of me, whatever ideas I had, always remaining friendly and calm.

We have now employed a new Head Gardener, Brendan Arundel, who came from RHS Hyde Hall and is highly qualified. Working alongside him are Chris Reeve, Graham Thorpe and (part-time) Katherine Johnson.

Chris Reeve

Chris is an experienced gardener with a huge knowledge of plants. He is especially brilliant at the pruning and training of roses, and is responsible for the Topiary Border, making even more out of it every year. He has single-handedly produced a book of wildlife at Helmingham, a subject about which he knows a great deal, as well as a plant guide that explains what is growing in every part of the garden. He drew the garden plan of Helmingham featured on pages 24–25 and has taken numerous skilled and sensitive photographs of plants, many of which are used in this book.

Graham Thorpe

Graham arrived on his bike one day asking if he could have a job – not knowing that we had just put an advert in the paper. We were impressed with his courage in coming up, and equally with the letter he handed in. He was a very young man then, but keen to learn, and he has worked in all areas of the garden. He also is getting more confident with the topiary and is responsible for the Snowman in particular.

Katherine Johnson

Katherine may be part-time, but she is invaluable in the amount of work which she seems to accomplish. (She told me she swims for a mile every week, which accounts for her strength and stamina!)

In the past we were lucky enough to have some volunteers from Otley College where they were taking garden design or horticulture courses. They had to do practical days as part of their course and at Helmingham they had the full range of experiences: dealing with trees, shrubs, herbaceous borders, roses, lawns, greenhouses, wild flowers, meadows, orchards, pruning, sowing and propagating.

We are always very grateful to have volunteers, and at the moment we have three wonderful people who are, respectively, retired, keen for a career change, and, as a result of the Covid pandemic, finding themselves with no work.

As for myself, I will be doing what I can for as long as I can. I adored working in the garden and was there most weekends. During the week I am usually very busy with my garden design business, travelling to and from projects, or on charity work, which takes up a lot of time. I am very involved with the RHS (and they work me hard!). And now, of course, I also have my own new garden at Framsden to care for.

All the same, the lure of Helmingham is hard to resist. I was very pleased when my son and daughter-in-law encouraged me to retain my involvement with the garden. Often on Sundays, when the garden is open, I am to be found under a rose bush or at some other task and people ask me if I work here. I always say yes – because it's true. (They sometimes also ask me how long I have worked here and I say forty-odd years and they say that they think the family must be very kind.)

RECIPES

We could happily – if not quite comfortably – live off the estate and farm and garden.

We did try to eat the pike once, when Tim gave me a Magimix and one of the first recipes I spotted was for *quenelles de brochet*.

Tim caught the pike quite easily, but deboning it was a nightmare for a very amateurish cook. Then I pulverized it in this wonderful new machine and made quenelles – small egg-shaped bundles of pike mixture – ready to poach. The Nantua sauce was a breeze and came out tasting delicious. Poaching the quenelles was easy. Eating them was a different matter: they tasted of moat mud.

We do eat venison, finding the saddle of fallow deer the best and tenderest of all.

But by far our favourites from the park are the little Soay sheep. Originally from the Norsemen, they settled in the island of Soay in the Hebrides. My father-in-law

Soay sheep in the park

introduced them to the park in the 1950s. We cull them as lambs in late August and I usually have about eight in the freezer. They are small but so delicious, not being as fatty as, for instance, Welsh lamb, and having darker-coloured meat.

The saddles feed at the most four people, so when my hungry family come, I usually roast two legs, which will feed ten to twelve people. The shoulders are smaller (not to mention difficult to carve), but I have found an easy way to use them.

Roy brings in large onions and big carrots. I wash the carrots but do not peel them. I chop these vegetables up roughly and quickly fry them in oil. I then rub the lamb with garlic, or shove a whole garlic bulb into the pot. I cut sprigs of rosemary from the Herb Garden outside and lay them on the veg. I seal the lamb in oil and then put it on top. I pour half a bottle of cheap red wine on to the mixture and about the same amount of stock. I cook the lamb in the top-right oven of the Aga for thirty minutes and then put it in the bottom-left oven, which is the plate-warming oven. I then forget it for four to five hours.

When I am ready I lift it out, put it on a carving dish and shove it in the hot oven to brown and crisp up for five to ten minutes. I strain the juices and thicken with *beurre manié* or cornflour, and serve it with a lovely green salad or winter veg.

We tried to eat one of the Highland cattle once. My parents-in-law had one butchered and I agreed to share it with them. When it was back from the butcher my mother-in-law told me to come and collect it. The meat covered the very large kitchen table and all the bags were named with titles I never knew existed, like star steak and brisket. The mince alone came to 36 kg/80 lb and that was just what was left over from everything else. We did not repeat the exercise!

We eat game from the shoots, pheasant and partridge, and trout that my husband brings back from his fishing trips.

Looking after a large working kitchen garden, we obviously had a lot of vegetables and fruit. I have already described how we have cut down the enormous amount of produce to reduce the workload and also because we were no longer feeding a large household. The amount we have now is about right, with the Coach House tea rooms taking salad crops and selling fresh vegetables in the gift shop. The rest of the vegetables and fruit come into the house and get used up.

I used to think that, with the produce of the kitchen garden combined with the venison and lamb and eggs from the chickens, we could feed a large houseful for quite some time without buying anything.

Early new potatoes, tiny baby carrots, peas and broad beans with herbs can be a wonderful fresh starter with a mousseline sauce.

I use beetroot for a hot vegetable, and cold for salads. We eat a lot of this and when we don't really want to see it on our salad plate any more, I make borscht, following this recipe that I learned from a Danish cousin.

Heat beef consommé up in a saucepan and put in minced cooked beetroot and let it stew (but never boil – boiling makes the soup sour) for twenty minutes. Strain it off, thicken with arrowroot and then add white wine vinegar and sherry to taste. It is delicious cold or hot and I serve it with crême fraîche or soured cream.

The peas were planted at fortnightly intervals so that we didn't have a glut. We used them either fresh or frozen (at any rate, what was left when they had been raided by the children). The broad beans were sown in both the autumn and the spring and the lettuce also. The runner beans were grown up the tunnels, rotating round the four tunnels. All the brassicas have to be protected from pigeons by netting. Leeks are always popular for a winter vegetable and for leek and potato soup.

Other favourites are artichokes. Our particular plants were brought over from Italy by my mother-in-law's parents, and they still thrive. We have given them away to friends and we have them now in our new home. I serve them hot or cold and if I have a lot, serve the artichoke bases with arancini and a hollandaise sauce.

ABOVE: Morello cherries growing on the north wall
BELOW FAR LEFT: Maincrop onions laid out to ripen
BELOW LEFT: A close-up of the Morello cherries

Tomatoes are grown inside the greenhouse for their early maturity (and I love the smell of the emerging leaves in the early spring); but the better-tasting ones are grown outside later in the year. Tomato salads with home-grown basil or red onions are sensational. Sweetcorn and asparagus are firm favourites and we have a very prolific salad crop both in the beds and the Potager.

We also have strawberries, raspberries and the three types of currant, black, red and white. Gooseberries are grown traditionally and also decoratively as standards.

The mulberry tree produces wonderful fruit, turns white T-shirts into red ones (permanently) and leaves telltale red marks round the lips. You know where the children have been.

Mulberry vodka is delicious, which is just as well, as I have failed miserably with making jam: the fruit is low in pectin and doesn't set. I have, however, had success with quince jelly – and, again, vodka made from this heavily scented and flavoured fruit is popular.

I made different-flavoured vodkas for Selina's wedding, using strawberry, raspberry and summer fruits, and then made the alcohol-soaked fruit into a very drunken pudding or ice cream. (Friends went to bed feeling pretty tipsy after it.)

More and more people are into growing their own vegetables and are eating more and more unusual vegetables and salads. We like to use heartsease and nasturtium leaves to decorate a salad. Daylily (*Hemerocallis*) leaves are also delicious, and each variety tastes slightly different. Blackcurrant leaf ice is a favourite to make before the fruit appears.

I very often have a stock pot on the go, with a left-over chicken carcass plus leeks, onions, carrots, parsnips and handfuls of herbs. There is very little wastage and what there is goes into the park to feed the deer. Apples and carrots go to the horses.

There is nothing much better than going into the garden and eating a handful of sun-warmed strawberries, or plucking a warm nectarine off the wall, or diving into the forest of dense fig leaves to find a cluster of ripe brown fruit.

I think that much of the charm and magic of Helmingham lies in the fact that it is a working garden, still relying on many of the tools that were used in the past. We are also mainly organic. I love working in the kitchen and making use of all our produce in different ways.

FLOWER CUTTING

I am not a flower arranger and do not have a cutting border as such, but I go around the garden bringing in a collection of flowers, grasses, foliage – in effect, bringing my garden into the house. This may be unorthodox but that's the natural way I like it. Daffodils, tulips, alliums, peonies, irises, roses, dahlias all to pick in abundance and then the plants like gaura (now *Oenothera lindheimeri*), giant scabious (*Cephalaria gigantea*) and *Bupleurum fruticosum*, and the grasses in their time. There is always something to pick and enjoy inside.

POTS

Planting pots is a growing hobby of mine – and, I see, of other gardeners. It's amazing what you can stuff into a pot and it all comes up and looks great.

I use the bulb lasagne described by Sarah Raven, planting tulips deep down in the pot, perhaps two different kinds, and then a layer of narcissi, and finally the crocus – the first to flower – on top.

For the summer, I was introduced by fellow gardener Fiona Lansdowne to *Pelargonium* 'Mystery', which has had many babies and is a consistent flowerer in big pots. Then there is the magic *P.* 'Lord Bute' and these both go very well with the fuchsia 'Lye's Unique', which is the only fuchsia I like for pots. This mixture might have a *Plectranthus argentatus* spilling out, with its grey leaves and long, elegant purple flowers. A chaenostoma, brachyscome or trailing geranium can be introduced to trail down. I also use helichrysum and heliotrope (the old-fashioned Cherry Pie).

I was so happy one year to grow *Iochroma australe*, a lovely plant with lavender-blue flowers. Proudly, I took one to the Great Dixter Flower Show to give to my friend Fergus Garrett. Having deposited my tiny offering in a minute pot, I then went around the garden, going of course into the Exotic Garden, where I found the same plant but about 2 metres/7 feet high and resembling a magnificent blue fountain. I felt suitably humbled.

Argyranthemum is also a very valuable plant, flowering for up to six months, and I plant several

varieties both in pots and to fill any gaps in the borders. And whatever you think of petunias, they flower their socks off and now come in really lovely pastel colours. The Tidal Wave series is amazing.

GREENHOUSES

The greenhouses at Helmingham are not showcases, they are working greenhouses and tucked away from the main gardens. Here we grow plants for the house which we also have for sale in the summer. For any big event I would drive the tractor and trailer up to the greenhouses to collect plants to embellish the house. There would be ferns for the dark areas and otherwise anything looking good to place throughout the house. Each bedroom had a flowering pot plant and a posy. As many parts of Helmingham are quite dark, I had to drive all these plants back to the greenhouses on a Monday morning.

I raise unusual plants and Chris is very good at looking after them. When I go on holiday, I always try to bring back seeds of anything interesting (I used to put cuttings into my sponge bag but that is no longer allowed). We have a propagator to bring on seeds and cuttings and a cold frame to harden certain plants off.

Among the usual selection, such as our early tomatoes, I have hibiscus brought back from Mexico, a great-great-grandchild of seeds of an acacia brought from Oman, a *Mimulus aurantiacus* that I had for my first Chelsea show garden (it had recently been given to me by Henry Keswick), and a sparrmannia plant which gets to an enormous height and looks sensational in the Great Hall. My collection also includes *Begonia luxurians*, *Streptocarpus* 'White Butterfly' and a charming *Begonia fuchsioides* which flowers for ever.

In the grapehouse Tim grows two varieties of grape, 'Black Hamburg' and the white 'Muscat of Alexandria'.

BELOW LEFT: *Dahlia* 'Faith'
BELOW CENTRE: A row of mixed dahlias
BELOW RIGHT: A combination of *Pelargonium* 'Mystery', *Plectranthus argentatus*, heliotrope, helichrysum and chaenostoma making a fine display in a big pot

A SEASONAL CALENDAR FOR THE HELMINGHAM GARDENS

SPRING JOBS

FEBRUARY

- Sow peas in early February if conditions are favourable; successive sowings to be made after previous ones have germinated (usually at fortnightly intervals).
- In mid-February chit early potatoes by setting, eyes upwards, in trays in a frost-free greenhouse or similar building, for approximately six weeks.
- Prepare ground for vegetables by raking previously dug beds to form a good tilth and a level seedbed.
- Prune bush roses, removing any dead and weak growth; cut back remaining strong growth by two-thirds to an outward-facing bud. We prune all the roses trained on the Helmingham Rose Support at this time.

MARCH

- Remove weeds by hoeing when conditions are favourable. If soil is dry and sun is shining, small weeds left on the surface will wilt and die, so removing won't be necessary.
- Repair any lawn damage with new turves or seed, using a half-moon edging tool to cut around the area to be turfed. After cutting, use a turfing iron to lift away damaged turf, slightly roughen area to be turfed with a rake and place new turf, making sure it is level with the surrounding area.
- Direct-sow seeds of hardy annual flowers such as poppies, convolvulus, linum.
- In the greenhouse sow half-hardies such as cosmos, nicotiana, antirrhinum, ageratum and, of course, our ornamental gourds.
- Sow broad beans early March, second sowing to be made after first sowing has germinated.
- Sow lettuce and salad crops at two-to-three-week intervals. If using cloches first sowings can be made in early March.
- This month we sow the seeds for our potager: millet, mizuna, beetroot 'Bull's Blood' and parsley.
- Other vegetable sowings to be made from March onwards include carrots, beetroot, parsnips, onions, leeks, spinach.
- The seed of brassicas – including cabbage, broccoli, cauliflower and Brussels sprouts – should all be sown now in a nursery bed, to be transplanted into final position later.
- Plant out early potatoes previously chitted.

APRIL

- Sow runner beans mid- to end April onwards.
- Lift overwintered brassica crops,
- Dig ground and prepare for maincrop potatoes.
- Plant dahlia tubers, staking and labelling named varieties.
- Support early-flowering perennials, such as poppies, with pea sticks, peonies with wire plant supports, irises with single-ring supports.
- Cut flowering heads of narcissus, tulips and hyacinth bulbs as foliage begins to turn yellow.
- Plant in final position (in our case up our tunnels) sweet peas which have been overwintered in a cold frame. Tie in with raffia as plants grow. Remove side-shoots and tendrils to gain height.
- Protect soft fruit by netting to stop birds damaging the crop.
- Hoe through all the borders, removing weeds. Apply fertilizer.
- Feed any young ornamental trees and clear weeds from base. Mulch if required.
- Cut down any deciduous grasses that have been left for winter interest and wildlife.
- Feed all roses with a good rose food.

The Main Border of the Walled Garden at midsummer

SUMMER JOBS

MAY–JUNE

- When the danger of frost has receded, usually by mid- to end May, plant half-hardy annuals.
- Plant up any pots now for summer flowering, mixing soil with slow-release fertilizer before planting. Keep well watered.
- Deadhead repeat-flowering roses. We feed the repeat-flowering roses every six to eight weeks to help them flower until early autumn.
- Deadhead perennials as and when necessary to prevent borders from looking tired. Remove annual poppies when over.
- Cut down any perennial poppies to ground level and fill gaps with container-grown plants: dahlias, lilies, French marigolds and tender salvias.
- Stake vulnerable flower plants with twiggy sticks, being careful not to leave too much of sticks showing above the plants. (Alternatively, trim down the sticks.)
- By mid-May you can carry out the Chelsea chop on any plants that respond well. We treat *Campanula lactiflora* in this way.

JULY–AUGUST

- In July, summer-prune trained fruit trees on walls: plums, gages, peaches, nectarines, pears and apples.
- Prune espalier pears and apples by cutting back outward-facing growth to two buds of the new season's growth. Tie in laterals, cut out any dead wood and replace with suitable new lateral. Prune laterals by one-third of new growth.
- In July lift irises that need dividing, then save only plump rhizomes, carefully cutting with sharp knife the young plump rhizome from the old and discarding the old. Trim back roots of new rhizomes to about 7–8 cm/3–3¼ inches and replant, leaving rhizome above ground with roots covered and growing. Plant rhizomes facing south to allow sun to bake them.

FAR LEFT: *Papaver somniferum* 'Black Beauty' with *Verbascum chaixii* 'Album'
CENTRE LEFT: *Agrostemma githago* 'Ocean Pearl' with a self-seeded poppy
NEAR LEFT: *Tulipa* 'Abu Hassan'
ABOVE: *Helenium* 'Moorheim Beauty', *Ammi majus* and *Lythrum salicaria* flowering together in the Main Border in late summer

- Take cuttings of pelargoniums, heliotropes and penstemons. Using a sharp knife, cut directly under a leaf joint; trim lower leaves off; then pot up in well-draining compost, making sure each cutting is firmly planted. For pelargoniums leave cuttings uncovered, for heliotropes and penstemons cover with plastic bag, supporting bag with small canes or sticks. This can also be done in early autumn.
- Trim box hedges and topiary with sharp shears. Trim yew and hornbeam hedges with shears or mechanical trimmer. This is normal practice, but in the last two years we experimented by trimming the box earlier, at the end of March. This avoids any scorching of new growth if it is very hot and also it is tough enough by the winter to avoid frost damage. So far it has worked.
- Using a reciprocating-blade mower, mow wildflower meadow at the end of August. Leave mown material for seven to ten days to allow seed to ripen and shed. Then clear all the mowings from the meadow and scarify some areas to encourage seed to germinate.
- This is the time we strim the moat banks.
- Keeping any recently planted young trees regularly watered with two or three buckets each twice a week is more beneficial than a sprinkler more often.

AUTUMN JOBS

SEPTEMBER–NOVEMBER

- In early September, take cuttings of pelargoniums, heliotropes and penstemons (if not already done).
- Mid-September is a good time to prepare seedbeds for overwintering lettuce. Once the lettuces have germinated, protect by covering with cloches or polythene but ventilate regularly to avoid botrytis (grey mould).
- Lift potatoes and store in a cool, dry, frost-free place. Cover with sacking or similar material to prevent tubers from turning green.
- Lift carrots and beetroot, saving only sound ones. Store in sand, placing carrots in layers, tops outermost, to protect from frost. Beetroot may be stored in the same way.
- Cut down herbaceous borders, selectively. Remove annuals and discard. Lift tender plants such as dahlias, pelargoniums, salvias, cannas, then store in a frost-free place. Remove plants from pots, refresh soil and mix in slow-release fertilizer for the bulbs to be planted.
- Prune climbing roses, removing old growth and replacing with strong young growth. Tie on, forming a fan shape. If insufficient young shoots, retain the best of the previous year's growth and prune side-shoots to two to three buds.
- Lift any perennial plants that need dividing, saving only growth from the outside of the clump before replanting.
- Divide any large perennials by using two forks back-to-back, gently prising handles apart.
- Fork over areas to be replanted, incorporating leafmould plus a sprinkling of bonemeal.
- Spread leafmould (plus any ash from bonfires) over the remainder of the border, using a digging fork between plants and removing any weeds.
- Having cleared vegetable plots of spent crops, apply manure or any organic matter ready for digging.
- When digging, remove trench at one end of the plot and take it to the other end, ready to back-fill when the plot has been dug.
- Lift summer bedding and prepare for spring-flowering plants and bulbs such as wallflowers and tulips.
- A useful tip for planting bulbs on cultivated land is to use a dibber; this is much quicker than using a trowel and it does not clog up as much. Use a bulb planter on grassland.
- Take hardwood cuttings of buddleia, lavender, philadelphus and viburnum.
- Prepare seedbed and in early November sow broad beans for overwintering.

Old rollers at the top of the Apple Walk, in autumn

WINTER JOBS

DECEMBER–JANUARY

- Dig any land not already dug to allow winter frosts to penetrate. This will aid the process of breaking down the soil for planting in spring, and also help to kill off undesirable pests.
- Prune raspberries, removing old canes (those which have fruited during summer), plus any weak growth. Tie in strong young new season's growth.
- Autumn-fruiting raspberries should be cut down to approximately 6–8 cm/2½–3¼ inches off the ground. When new growth appears in spring and summer for autumn fruiting, tie in as necessary.
- Prune standard apple trees, removing any dead wood and any growth which crosses over the other branches, the aim being to ensure the tree has the shape of a cup, with the centre of the tree open to allow in sunlight, which will improve the quality of the fruit. Prune leader shoots back by two-thirds, side-shoots to two to three buds. Always prune to an outward- and upward-pointing bud.
- In the greenhouse, pot on any rooted cuttings, such as pelargoniums, heliotropes, penstemons.
- Divide dahlia tubers ready to pot up in spring.
- Cut hazels for pea sticks, tying in bundles of 2–3 metre/7–10 foot lengths, which can then be cut to desired lengths as needed in spring. Any straight lengths of hazel should be saved and used as stabilizers for supporting tall-growing perennials.
- Clear up fallen leaves and save for turning into leafmould. A good method of making leafmould is to pack leaves into plastic bags – old compost bags or similar – and tie the tops, then stack the bags in layers. This speeds up the breaking-down process.
- Wash down greenhouses with detergent, including both glass and floors. Also wash pots and seed trays in the same way.
- Make exciting plans for the next year, sitting by the fire!

RECOMMENDED SEED VARIETIES USED AT HELMINGHAM

Tomatoes: F1 hybrid 'Shirley', 'Sweet 100'
Early potatoes: Premier', 'Charlotte', 'Foremost'
Maincrop: 'Majestic' (grown also for its lovely white flowers)
Peas: 'Twinkle'
Broad beans: 'Crimson-flowered'
Broad beans for overwintering: 'Aquadulce Claudia'
Runner beans: ' Painted Lady', 'White Lady', 'Scarlet Emperor'
Gourds: 'Small-Fruited Mix'
Lettuce for overwintering: 'Valdor'
Artichokes: Ours are an old variety brought over from Italy in the 1940s.

Of course we grow many other vegetable varieties as well, but these are the ones we feel most confident in recommending.

Tunnel in snow

LIVING AND GARDENING AT HELMINGHAM

Living and gardening at Helmingham has been a terrific adventure and a steep learning curve. Above all, Helmingham was and is a very happy family home. As to the garden, it is true that one never stops learning.

To work in the garden for a whole day does wonders for my state of mind. Mental health has been on everyone's radar in the time of the Covid pandemic, but I can say, with hand on heart, that I come in at the end of a day in the garden tired, rewarded and feeling great satisfaction and enormous happiness.

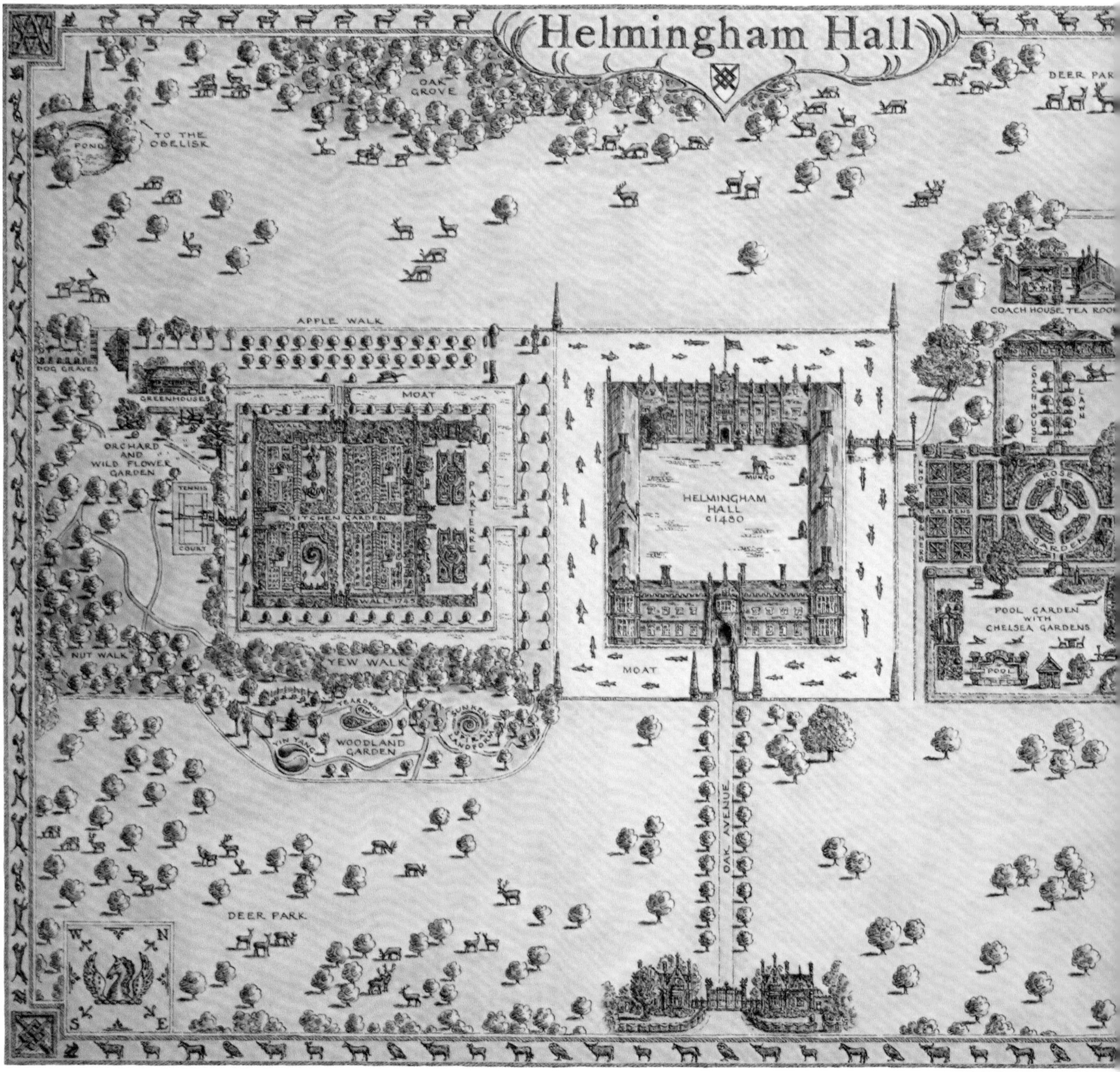

I hope many others can share these experiences, whether they are lucky enough to have a big garden like ours or have only a a small plot or a window box.

Helmingham has provided me with the confidence to take on a new career, which is the next part of this book – but you haven't heard the last from me, because I am now creating a new garden which is featured at the end.

Julia Bickham, *Helmingham Hall*, a gift from my son James and his wife, Florrie

THE BUSINESS

My parents-in-law tentatively opened the garden in the early 1970s, with an honesty box at the garden gate. They also made a small tea room in the Coach House. We all had great pleasure in seeing people go around the Walled Garden.

As the garden grew so did the number of visitors, and, of course, by 1982 we had planted the gardens on the other side of the house. There was a huge new area to be explored and so we started to increase the garden-opening business.

We introduced a pay-box halfway up the drive, where we would welcome the visitors, whose numbers increased year by year. I opened a small shop in the stable yard, which I ran for some five years, but I was not a good shopkeeper, buying items which were too expensive from the Birmingham trade fair every year. It didn't make much profit, so this was taken over by our secretary, Jane – and became much more profitable as a result!

We also turned the rather decrepit Coach House into a much smarter tea room, lining the high walls with huge trellis arched panels and putting a proper kitchen at the back.

As the garden established, we realized that this was a good business opportunity and that we needed publicity. I invited journalists over to see the garden and over the next ten years I had big features in the *East Anglian Daily Times*, followed by wonderful articles in *Country Life*, *Gardens Illustrated*, the *Daily Telegraph* magazine and *The English Garden*, as well as the RHS *Garden* magazine.

By 1996 my dressage career had come to an end and so the stables were slowly requisitioned for shop storage. One or two other little shops run by others then materialized.

Charles Loyd, our agent, brilliantly suggested to us that we could hold a vintage Bentley rally. In its first year, 2008, about twenty of these wonderful cars turned up and we had a welcoming dinner for them (well, for their owners and drivers). Charles then started to expand this and it has become a main event in the garden calendar. Now, every year, thousands of cars and visitors flock to Helmingham's Festival of Classic and Sports Cars.

When I was approached by Plant Heritage to have a plant fair, I happily agreed. This is run by Jim and Sarah Marshall and in 2010 we had ten stalls in the courtyard. Now, more than ten years later, we hold two major events a year, with a Spring and Autumn Plant Fair, each of them an extremely happy and successful event that attracts small specialist nurseries from all over the UK and further afield.

I had been to the famous Courson plant fair in France and I was bowled over by wonderful nurseries turning up and simply putting their plants in boxes on the ground. Eager gardeners, both local enthusiasts and elegant Frenchwomen in beautiful couture clothes, milled around, and had delicious food and drink in the various marquees. I dreamed of having such an event at Helmingham and I can honestly say we now do. It has a very special atmosphere.

As these events grew we realized we needed an events manager and so we employed Katy, who, with her

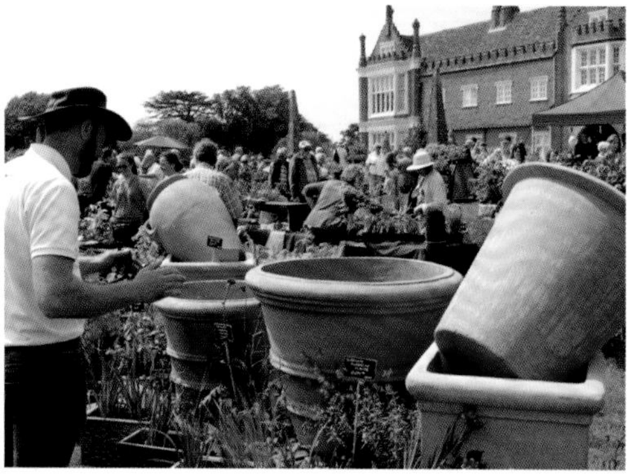

FAR LEFT: The Plant Heritage Fair
LEFT: The Festival of Classic and Sports Cars
OPPOSITE: The wrought-iron gate at the top of the Walled Garden

fantastic enthusiasm and help, has been instrumental in increasing the business – which now includes an Artisan Market that accompanies the Plant Fair.

We started having weddings in the Coach House and that has progressed into one almost every weekend, either in a marquee in the park or on the Parterre or in the Coach House.

Although the house is private, it is, clearly, a major asset and we began to think of more ways of using it and yet retaining it as a private family home. A great friend introduced me to Tom Savage, the Director of the Winterthur Museum in Delaware, who takes tours round the UK, staying in wonderful houses. While I was in New York I met him for dinner and we hit it off. He arranged two lecture tours for me in the US and for several years running brought a party of art enthusiasts to stay at Helmingham

These visits were hard work – my ambition, which I pretty much managed, was to feed them entirely from the estate – but huge fun. It was a win-win situation as they were all charming and lovely and we could show Helmingham off, but as a private home. I have remained great friends with Tom ever since – and perhaps he will come back again?

I tried to hold operas in the garden, but however beguiling an idea, in practice it was a disaster. One particular evening, with *La Bohème* half-way through, the wind got up and the rain came in horizontally. When they got to the bit where Rudolfo sings, 'Your tiny hand is frozen' and lights a candle, the candle swiftly went out. Gales of laughter from the equally frozen crowd. Then the very slight, skinny pianist suddenly got up and ran into the house. I followed him, took him into the drawing room where there was a roaring fire, and wrapped him up in a cashmere rug. Going out, with help from our house guests, we took rugs and coats to keep people warm. To roars of applause, the pianist came back and we finished the opera. Never again!

Katy by then was in her stride and she enlarged the shop considerably and did away with the halfway house paybox. I had a notion of opening an ice cream parlour and eventually we were able to do it and put it in another stable next to the shop. This has proved to be a great success and very popular (especially with my grandchildren, and also my husband).

Katy had the brainwave of having Music in the Garden and we now have several lovely Sunday evenings with music of differing genres on the Parterre and people bring their picnics. One memorable evening I brought Mungo, my Rhodesian Ridgeback, out to greet people. I had Mungo on a lead, but my husband's naughty cocker spaniel, Maestro, escaped and caught up with me. For Maestro, it was too much of a temptation to have a lovely wicker picnic basket lying on the ground; to my horror, I saw him lift his leg against it. (Fortunately the guests had finished their picnic and, kindly, they appeared unaware of the Maestro's urges.)

Now our son Edward and his wife, Sophie, are in control and moving the business on with Katy, who by now has an assistant, Sam. They are full of energy and ideas and it is heartening to see the business growing by the day. In particular the Garden Illuminations, held before Christmas, where the gardens are all lit up, is proving to be a massive hit.

CHELSEA FLOWER SHOW 1997

CLASSICAL CALM WITH A TOUCH OF TOMORROW

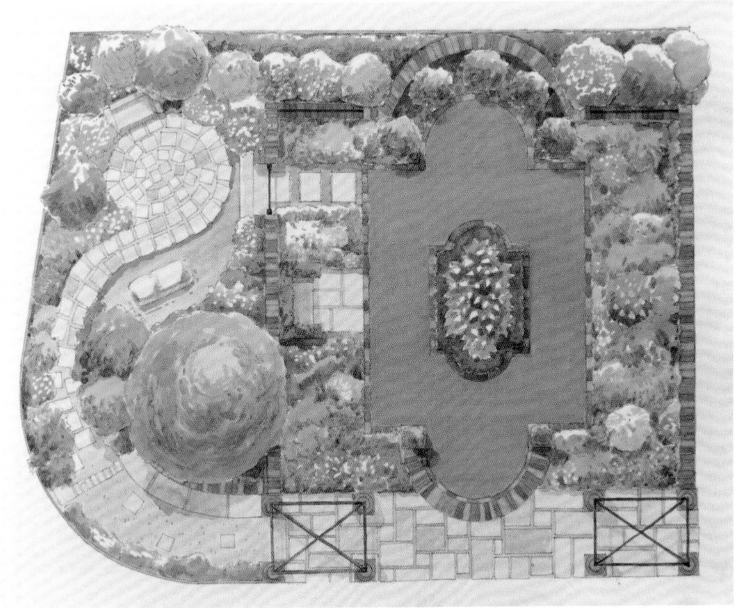

ABOVE: The plan of the garden

I started my career as a professional garden designer in 1996 – rather late in my life, as until then I had been a busy housewife and mother, and also a very competitive dressage rider. (I had some courageous friends who had asked me to design their gardens before that, but – they were courageous!)

I began by taking drawing lessons from Jill Fenwick in Dorking: she had to start me from scratch, with learning how to do surveys, drawing to scale and axonometric drawing.

Anyway, the editor of the *Evening Standard*, Max Hastings, who had seen my garden at Helmingham, very bravely asked me to design a garden for the paper at the 1997 Chelsea Flower Show.

This was a big ask, as I really didn't have a clue how to go about it.

I asked friends about whether I should do it and they tended to say I shouldn't; my husband thought it was too huge a task and far too risky.

However, my son James, who was sixteen years old at the time, told me in no uncertain terms that I was always telling them to grab the challenges

OPPOSITE: The central bed of arum lilies (*Zantesdeschia aethiopica*)

in life when they came and not to shrink from anything that seemed too daunting and that I should jolly well practise what I preached. So there!

Rather abashed, I slunk away and went to visit a designer friend who had done many a Chelsea garden. She advised against it, pointing out the trials and tribulations that it inevitably involved, which immediately made me think that I must go along with James – and do it.

The next step was to meet Harry Davey, who would be project-managing the show garden for the *Evening Standard* and we went around the showground at the 1996 show. It all seemed absolutely terrifying but he was very reassuring.

I had asked Max Hastings to give me a brief for the garden and he just said to design something that people could relate to, which didn't give me much to go on. Especially as someone who, frankly, didn't have a clue what she was letting herself in for. However, my brother Freddie, a very successful events manager himself, suggested I should meet set designer Jon Kellett, who could really 'see' a space (and know what to do with it). Jon and I met at the showground and we toured round with the crowds and then retired to a lovely little Italian restaurant called Fontana in Lower Sloane Street, where we ordered a bottle of wine. By the time lunch was over, we had sketched the design on white paper napkins and we were all done. I tottered back to the flat and rang Max to say I would do it. He sounded delighted and promised me that the paper would help in any way they could. I then had about eleven months of sleepless nights.

I think that creating a Chelsea garden is rather like having a baby. You have three or four months of morning sickness, then a space of relative calm. It's then a three-week dash to prepare for this baby (or build this garden). One or two huge pushes and it's there. In the case of your Chelsea garden, you have polished every leaf and scrubbed every stone. Then the judges come along and tell you that there are too many buttons on the cardigan and the bootees don't match. But you think your baby/garden is the most beautiful thing in the world.

The build-up was at times exhilarating and at times agonizing. (Just as a help, the weather in England in mid-May is always testing – lashing rain or burning sun.)

To make the garden seem real, Jon suggested a fictitious couple who would live there. They were christened 'Henry' and 'Octavia'.

We had a formal terrace at the front of the garden with two sets of four classic brick columns tied in with swirling ironwork. Steps led down on to a lawn with double herbaceous borders either side, overflowing with flowers within brick walls clothed with climbing roses, clematis and trained *Exochorda* x *macrantha*. These borders were rich with roses, geraniums, campanulas and irises, and spiked with tall alliums. In the middle of the lawn was a brick-edged bed, planted with a dwarf box hedge and arum lilies. At the end of the garden we planted five *Sorbus aria* 'Lutescens', with behind them panels of ironwork, made by John Churchill, which were skilfully fashioned into replicas of the arum lilies; he also made a wonderful gate which linked the two sections of the garden. At the end of the show I had the two panels made into low gates, which are still at Helmingham (see photograph on page 64).

There was no doubt that the owner, 'Henry', would stand on the terrace with his colleagues, drinking a glass of champagne. On the other side of the wall was an informal woodland scene with stepping stones and a contemporary sculpture by Louise Gardiner, and here his wife, 'Octavia', would prance around in bare feet, worshipping the sun. The dominant plants in this part of the garden were masses of blue poppies (*Meconopsis*), ferns and foxgloves.

Anyway, it was the most wonderful experience and the best thing about it was the camaraderie of everyone on site: fellow garden designers were very helpful and would let you have their spare pile of soil (and you spared your digger for an hour). The RHS staff were encouraging and informative and cheered you up.

I learned it was important to finish the planting by the Saturday, as the photographers come around then. The assessors come on the Sunday. These terrifying people are there to assess everything and spend time in the garden before the judges arrive on the Monday. They look to see how true the garden is to the brief; they inspect the building and the finish. They examine the plants to make sure they are all correctly planted in the right place; and the garden mustn't be crowded. Finally, when they have picked it all to pieces they give their opinion as to what medal might be given, although the final choice is for the judges (who in those days had to be finished by lunch on Judgment Day, so didn't have the time to be so thorough).

On either side of the central bed, borders planted with campanulas, nepeta, roses and alliums; on the left a box-edged seat

My team were absolutely wonderful: the contractor Mike Chewter; the plantsman and nurseryman David Howard; John Churchill, the artist who made the ironwork; Bulmer Brick and Tile Co. from Suffolk, who made the pillars; Mattocks the rose growers; Ruskins, who provided the trees and hedging; Louise Gardiner, who created the wonderful contemporary sculpture, and Alexander Macdonald-Buchanan with his terracotta pots (which set him off on a meteoric career). The help from the *Evening Standard* was superb: I was supported at every step. Jon Kellett was invaluable in making the design work.

I am so grateful to have been given the chance to create a Chelsea Flower Show garden – and, as it happened, it all came good and I got a Gold Medal!

I have a private garden at Helmingham with booty from my three Chelsea gardens and I resurrected four of the classic brick columns for this little garden, which we call the Chelsea garden.

A friend overheard someone asking at the show, 'And who is Xa Tollemache?' and the answer from the other person was, 'Oh, she is just an amateur.'

I had to laugh, because it was so true.

DUNBEATH CASTLE

CAITHNESS

ABOVE: The castle illuminated at dusk, down the keyhole driveway

I took the sleeper train to Inverness and then hired a car to get my first view of this wonderfully romantic seventeenth-century castle. It is perched up high on a clifftop in the most northerly mainland county of Caithness, about as far north as you can possibly go.

The Clan Sinclair owned the estate from 1452 to 1945 and it is now owned by Tertius and Claire Murray-Threipland, distant relatives. From the little harbour of Dunbeath you see the castle glistening white across the water, teetering on top of the cliff.

Approaching it is another adventure. In the nineteenth century David Bryce remodelled and landscaped the spectacular entrance drive. Entering past the lodge there are tantalizing glimpses of the front of the castle, some half a mile away. This is known as a keyhole driveway and as you descend the full sight of the castle appears and the Moray Firth behind it. It is a pretty spectacular sight.

There are two walled gardens, one on either side of the drive, behind rows of sycamores bent over by the winds which blow at 100 mph and from every direction.

OPPOSITE: The view to the castle from the Southern Walled Garden, which is hedged with *Rosa rugosa* 'Alba' and planted with blocks of campanulas

The Southern Walled Garden (to the right of the drive) was first laid out in 1860 and has had a few facelifts since then. I was asked to come here in 1998 to remodel this particular garden. This large space of nearly a hectare/ 2 acres was enclosed by a high stone wall which we entered through a small gate a short walk up from the castle, although there is a service access at the other end. It has two raised lookouts in corners and rather wonderful greenhouses at the top.

A double herbaceous border marched up the centre on either side of a grass path, but the working areas were in a dreadful state and had wire fences that were falling down and a cold frame in the middle of one of the beds. I remember thinking this garden was a lost soul of faded beauty.

I absolutely didn't want to change the feeling of space, but the garden needed structure. So I designed several small gardens, each providing a different service and personality, yet not distracting from the vastness of the place. This was to be a beautiful, well-designed garden combining flowers, fruit, vegetables, herbs and tender ornamentals. The owners brought back interesting art objects from the Far East to place in some areas.

We made two vegetable gardens, a working one for use in the castle kitchen and the other a decorative space showing how the flowers, foliage and texture of vegetables can look so lovely – for example, an artichoke against a row of bold Tuscan kale, with tall purple alliums spiking the borders. Different-coloured kales also add to the fun.

OPPOSITE: A view from one of the raised lookouts on to the finished garden
RIGHT: A tall, narrow gateway leading to the castle
BELOW: A Caithness slate sundial and some showy kales

LEFT: The main border, with campanulas in show-off mood
OPPOSITE: A Chinese sculpture, ringed with kniphofias, dianthus and David Austin roses

We planted a cutting garden and a rose garden (learning from experience that only the low-growing David Austin roses were able to survive the lashing winds). Fruit is grown for the house and is also trained into attractive shapes. We also planted a *Fuchsia* 'Riccartonii' hedge all the way around the garden, leaving wide grass paths around the perimeter and narrow borders against the walls. This is a very tough hedge, which can withstand the dramatic weather conditions – and it looks very Scottish.

We introduced tunnels of deciduous planting to separate the various spaces and I made a little water feature in one corner, using pebbles from the beach and a lead container with a pump housed in a small ironwork structure. There were obelisks of ironwork, painted in Dunbeath Blue, for the sweet peas which we planted to prolong the flowering season. I wish it had been my idea, but I have to confess that it was my client who put ballcocks from old loos, painted gold, on top of the obelisks. They look so grand!

The long greenhouse was bursting with colour and interesting tender plants when I last saw it. A warm welcome to greet you at the top of the garden.

On one of my visits, Claire asked me to have a few thoughts about the Northern Walled Garden (to the left of the drive), which was also in an awful condition at the time. There was a charming old laundry building, which I believe is now used for entertaining. I designed a modern reflective pool and, as water features, I put some old Caithness flagstone containers previously used for collecting rainwater for the laundry. However, Tertius then enthusiastically took over this garden and has created a completely different space from across the drive, with a mass planting of grasses, streams, water and buildings. I think it is stunning.

When I first went to Dunbeath Claire was not confident of planting or plants, but, as time went on, she became passionate about the garden. When I last went back, I could see how, with her input, it had become her garden and not mine. She had the invaluable help of Neil Millman, who has introduced interesting new planting: and it is thought that there are some three thousand different species in the gardens now. Among the new plantings are cardiocrinum, anemonopsis, arisaema, and the white *Paeonia emodi*. How wonderful to think that this Himalayan peony and the amazing Himalayan blue poppy (*Meconopsis*) can thrive there. To Claire and Neil's credit they have taken the garden forward and added to the structure without disturbing it.

It's a funny thing about designing: I get so involved with the planning from the first stages, looking at the site, studying the levels, the climate and the drainage, and then getting the survey and starting to scribble and think about shapes and anything from the buildings that inspires me. When all these plans are approved, then I move on to plants, and by the time I have planted the last of the little scatterers in the beds, I am obsessed with it all and I find it very hard to walk away and not claim complete ownership! I have to remind myself that it is *not* my garden and that it will change and develop over the years – almost always for the better.

CASTLE HILL

DEVON

ABOVE: A painting of the garden
(by an artist whose name we have so far been unable to discover)

This beautiful, romantic place nestles in the quiet countryside of north Devon, overlooking a river which is a tributary of the Bray. It sits in a Grade I listed eighteenth-century park which sets off this wonderful Palladian house built in 1730 by Hugh Fortescue.

Sadly, the centre block was destroyed by fire in 1934, but fortunately it was rebuilt in 1936 back to its original design and it is still lived in by the family. From the road you see the house, the colour of pale honey, sitting in the green contours of the many terraces which end at water cascades along the river. Beyond is the designed landscape of carefully planted trees which allow a final view of the Triumphal Arch on the horizon. This clever and elegant planting was done by Hugh Fortescue, who became Earl Clinton. In 2005, invasive plants were cleared to reveal the Holwell Temple further round the landscape.

The old castle sits behind and high above the house; and in between is the famous Woodland Garden, with its planting of rhododendrons, magnolias, azaleas, cornus and many, many other acid-loving plants, both rare and well known. These include eucryphias, camellias, hydrangeas and acers,

OPPOSITE: The Millennium Garden, with *Quercus ilex* mopheads and *Lavandula* x *intermedia* 'Grosso'

and they are backed by magnificent beech trees planted 150 years ago, under which is a mass planting on a grand scale of daffodils. Spring bulbs herald the arrival of the early shrubs throughout the garden.

Tommy and Nell Arran have continued to plant this garden extensively and it is now a fitting testimony to their knowledge, enthusiasm and hard work over many years, supported by a very small team of hard-working gardeners.

In 1999, they asked me to design a summer garden to celebrate the new millennium. Their idea was to create colour and interest after the spring-flowering Woodland Garden had finished and before the arrival of autumn colour. This garden is on the west side of the house. You can catch glimpses as you approach the house, but it is shielded by a wide grass space planted with specific trees.

Rather oddly, when I go to a new site I always see first the things that appear wrong to me. However, often, when you live in a garden, these mistakes are not apparent simply because of familiarity. Here, it seemed that the energy of the present garden was wrong, the lines of the paths and borders curving in instead of out. Plus, there was a hideous bright blue swimming pool in the middle of the sweeping grass terraces leading to the historic water cascades. Not only that, but there was an ugly shed by the pool. A little monster.

I hesitated saying this but I suggested I could only design a garden for them if they filled in the pool and torched the hut. On my second visit, this had been done! Now I had to get going.

An initial sketch was done illustrating the general concept that we thought would suit the house. As my hero Russell Page always said, 'the garden should curtsey

OPPOSITE: The Millennium Garden border, with recent introductions of *Pyrus salicifolia*
ABOVE: The Millennium Seat, and beds edged by *Lavandula* x *intermedia* 'Grosso' in full bloom

to the house' and here it was essential to design a garden that didn't dominate either the house or the famous landscape but could, equally, stand up to them both.

So, in my design generous outward-lying borders were swept in to act like a giant shoulder for the house. You can imagine my delight when Nell showed me a picture by the eighteenth-century John Wootton which had the same shape and energy. The only difference was that in the picture there were great trees, while they wanted a summer garden with flowers and borders.

At the bottom of this sloping site was a space with a very decorative stone seat, there for the purpose of looking up to the right-hand façade of the house, which of course at that time you didn't see, because it was obscured by the planting.

Once the plan of the garden was approved, the diggers arrived. The old borders were cleared along with several large rhododendrons, revealing at last that part of the house.

I always look to the architecture of a house and use it for any inspiration for the design of the garden and here were great copper domes on the roof.

It was decided to plant a line of *Quercus ilex* to define the outward boundary of the garden, echoing Wootton's painting, but here I suggested they clip the trees into dome shapes to accentuate the roof domes.

To great excitement the trees arrived from Holland and they were really rather skinny (expensive though they had been to buy). But they were the right height and Nell was very encouraging, saying they would soon fill out, which of course they did after a year or two. I chose them because there were two very established holm oak trees already there, so I reckoned my skinny Dutch adolescents would survive the brutal winds of north Devon.

We had a few scares. The serpentine *Viburnum tinus* hedge that I planted underneath them got a ferocious virus and we had to think of something to replace it. I had planted a hedge of *Osmanthus* x *burkwoodii* at home and this was such a success that I reckoned it would be the perfect choice for here. It can be clipped to whatever size and it could be encouraged to curve in the right direction and generally behave itself. Added to this, it could face up to the elements.

I love this hedge. It is the difference between the very formal denseness of yew and a looser hedge like hornbeam. It is evergreen too and is just that nice mid-green, not the brightness of box but lighter and softer than yew. It also has scented white flowers in spring. So, we also chose it to replace the original hornbeam hedge that led you into the garden from the drive (the hornbeam had looked very unhappy there, so we replanted it in the Woodland Garden where it has since thrived). The osmanthus hedge curls round the back of a seat on the right of the drive looking on to this new Millennium Garden and then wraps round two holm oaks, leading you in.

A modern water sculpture by Giles Rayner appears in front of you, looking wonderful with this great house as a backdrop. Behind the sculpture is a repeat of the osmanthus and holm oak planting scheme, which creates continuity at the entrance.

Nell Arran's mother, who had previously lived in the house, gave her daughter a wonderful stone seat which they placed at the head of the garden against the house;

it is flanked by two lovely lead greyhounds. Steps edged with lavender lead you on to the garden path, taking you down to the bottom. This path is also edged with lavender. There was much thinking on the wisdom of planting lavender in rainy Devon, but I was advised that *Lavandula* x *intermedia* 'Grosso' was much more wet-tolerant than other varieties. In the main it has done well (though, admittedly, the plants in the lowest part of the garden did suffer with wet feet, despite endless gravelly bottoms).

Box hedging provided the outline of the top beds but this got the dreaded blight and was replaced after sixteen years with *Euonymus japonicus* 'Green Rocket'.

OPPOSITE: The newly visible façade of the house
BELOW: The view over the garden, with the sculpture by Giles Rayner, to the parkland

Within this formal outline, planting had to be done with care. The honey colour of the house didn't marry happily with pink, so I chose blues, purples, whites, creams and soft yellows, with dark red for depth. This Millennium Garden starts off with spring bulbs and finishes with dahlias and asters in huge groups. The significant plants are trained *Pyrus salicifolia* 'Pendula', their silver foliage making a lovely contrast to the evergreen oaks. In addition, to give height, we have clematis trained on my designed structural supports. There are large clumps of the pale *Agapanthus* 'Blue Moon', the feathery *Artemisia lactiflora* Guizhou Group, *Campanula lactiflora*, eupatorium and echinacea – and roses, which have been introduced relatively recently. Spring bulbs, especially tulips and alliums, provide a dazzling sight in early spring and summer.

It was important that the garden be large enough to be in proportion to the house and the landscape, and

also that it should have a certain level of formality: the oaks, the osmanthus, the euonymus and the lavender all contribute to this. At the same time, abundant informal planting within softens and enhances.

I think the right touch of modernity is very important to bring the garden into the present and this is represented here by the modern sculpture and the contemporary planting.

As William Kent so wisely said, 'Garden as though you will live forever.'

OPPOSITE, CLOCKWISE FROM TOP LEFT: *Agapanthus* 'Blue Moon'; *Thalictrum delavayi* and *T.* Splendide White; *Clematis* 'Polish Spirit'
RIGHT: *Salvia* (syn. *Perovskia)* 'Blue Spire'
BELOW: Newly planted *Euonymus* 'Green Rocket' at the top of the garden

CHOLMONDELEY CASTLE

CHESHIRE

ABOVE: The view over the lake towards the castle

It was in 2008 that Lavinia Cholmondeley rang me up and asked me to come and have a look at an overgrown area of the garden at Cholmondeley Castle.

This was pretty early in my new career, but I had visited the castle and gardens many times, as we have a dairy farm nearby and the Cholmondeleys were always kind to us. Lavinia and I used to go hunting together and she was a very fearless rider. I used to drive my horse from Suffolk to her stables, which then took about eight hours, and Terry, the groom, always had a nip of something for me when I arrived or after hunting, back in the yard. (It was usually a Whisky Mac.)

I was thrilled to be invited to look at the Duckery, as this part of the garden was called. It was so named because Lavinia's husband, Hugh, had kept a whole lot of ornamental wildfowl there. The space was filled by a large lake where his ducks thrived. He was very proud of them and would go down there to feed them whenever he was at home. Hugh had sadly died some years before and the Duckery was now a jungle. The rest of the

OPPOSITE: Cholmondeley Castle and its immediate grounds

large garden was already open to the public and much admired. So how was I going to create a new garden here in this overgrown area?

We walked to see it – a bit of a challenge, as the laurels came right down to the edge of the lake and it was thick with Japanese knotweed. This is a particularly ferocious beast, very difficult to get rid of. It was introduced to Europe by the German botanist Philipp von Siebold, who admired its beauty. The Royal Botanic Gardens at Kew received a shipment of it in 1850 and by the mid-1850s it was being sold commercially. No one was aware of the invasive nature of the plant until much later. The rest, as they say, is history.

It took us three years to get rid of it at Cholmondeley mainly by spraying and by cutting off the thickest stems and injecting weedkiller down the remaining stems. It eventually got weaker and weaker. Simultaneously, we were cutting down and removing a lot of laurels.

The wonderful part of this rather laborious exercise was that beautiful trees appeared from nowhere. Species rhododendrons and stunning cherries, oaks and chestnuts were at last visible and could be admired. It was a great start to making a new garden.

Lady C. was a formidable gardener: she had planted huge numbers of ornamental trees all over the garden and up into the woodland, and also created the Temple Garden, with its azaleas and ferns and cascades. There was already a Victorian sandstone temple on an island in the middle of a large pool. She added a second pool at the top of a restored rockery looking over the garden below and also created a rose garden and two big herbaceous borders designed by Randle Siddeley. The borders around the castle were formal and smart. She was a woman with extremely good and knowledgeable taste and was a very good friend.

I always feel that formality should be around the house and that increased informality should lead you to the wider landscape, and the Duckery was adjacent to the parkland. I think some members of the family were keen on creating a Japanese garden, but I felt it really should be a beautiful woodland walk, which was missing in this great garden, and so I said to Lavinia that if she wanted a Japanese garden, I was not the person to design it. Anyway, she agreed that it should be a plant-filled walk around the lake with simple woodland planting; a quiet, relaxed and peaceful area with seating. In addition, it had interesting elements in the Victorian water cascades, which needed complete restoration. This restoration work was done by the estate staff moving the rocks that had shifted, blocking the water flow. We arranged ferns and decorative trees and shrubs including *Cornus canadensis* around these lovely features. One of the cascades falls into a pond, and a small bridge takes you down past the island back into the main garden.

I drew up a rough plan which had a winding path with an entrance and an exit and other paths leading out of the garden and into different areas. We cut down large areas of laurel, leaving a shelter belt to protect the young plants.

But there was something missing and that was a focal point to catch your gaze as you arrived at the garden. Now by chance, I had recently completed a garden at the Chelsea Flower Show and, also just by chance, I had persuaded my husband to allow me to pull down a stretch of beautiful walling in our woods nearby to use for the show garden.

After the show it had to be taken off site and I managed to persuade Lady C. that all that was now required for the Duckery was a Gothic folly and that – just by chance – I had the local stone to build it. I rang up my friend and fellow garden designer George Carter, whom I work with on various projects, and he drew up a perfect Gothic folly which complemented the Gothic Cholmondeley Castle. He had a beautiful little picture done for Lady C., and that cemented the deal. We then went to various reclamation centres in search of some tracery to give it a monastic feel. To this day it looks as though it has been there for centuries.

It did not seem appropriate on this site to draw up a plan, so I started on the planting, putting together a substantial list of trees, shrubs and herbaceous plants for Lavinia's approval. We agreed on most things – except that I would say how much I loved amelanchier and that we needed a group of seven, to which she would reply, 'I think three will be enough, Xa.' I would then suggest a mass planting of euphorbias and she would say that she thought three would be a start! Anyway, we never fell out, and the garden began to take shape.

OPPOSITE, ABOVE: The Folly Garden
OPPOSITE, BELOW: Restored Victorian water cascades

OPPOSITE, CLOCKWISE FROM TOP LEFT: *Miscanthus sinensis* 'Morning Light' with *Alchemilla mollis*; *Leucojum aestivum* 'Gravetye Giant' with *Brunnera macrophylla* 'Jack Frost'; a planting of rhododendrons and ligularia on a site overlooking the island
LEFT: Siberian iris 'Perry's Blue'
BELOW: An old rhododendron with *Euphorbia griffithii* 'Dixter'

We planted cornus, acers, the white form of Himalayan birch (*Betula utilis* subsp. *jacquemontii*), magnolias and *Quercus palustris*, liquidambars, golden larches and amelanchiers, with a middle storey of bamboos, viburnums and hydrangeas and a lower storey of Siberian iris, grasses and hostas. With other ground cover, plants such as ferns and primulas fundamentally completed this garden. Masses of bulbs were planted and it became a pretty, peaceful garden that the visiting public came to love.

It is my greatest pleasure when one of my gardens progresses, and here there has been lots more planting done. More large areas of laurels were cleared and with Barry, the wonderful new head gardener, it has taken on a new lease of life, with masses more plants but much the same planting palette as I originally designed. It has not lost its character. On the contrary, there is much more to admire and see now. It has been greatly expanded.

Gardens hopefully evolve and here is a great example of that happening with the next generation coming in and enhancing them. As we know, gardens don't stay still, and they very often lose that intimacy and specialness when the owner dies. But in this case, I think Lavinia would be thrilled to see what the Duckery has turned into. (I am glad to say that it has been renamed the Folly Garden.)

BELOW: The meadow by the lakeside
OPPOSITE: The Folly, towering over new rhododendrons

BIGHTON HOUSE

HAMPSHIRE

ABOVE: View of the house over the lawn. The mighty urn has now been moved to provide a focal point at the end of the avenue, with added planting to embrace it.

This Victorian house sits in an elevated position overlooking rural Hampshire's rolling landscape, from which you don't see another house. It is an elegant yet unpretentious house with classical proportions.

I have known this house since 1996 and previously it had been a very happy family home, but after a divorce it had to be sold. The new owner kindly asked me, a very new designer, to do plans, starting with the Walled Garden at the east of the house. A very brave decision.

The garden was in a sorry state. The swimming pool was not only at very odd angles to the walls but actually had a dead fox floating around in it. Added to that, the tennis court was also in here, with a huge hornbeam hedge cutting the garden in half but diagonally, presumably to fit the court in! The vegetable garden and orchard were at the bottom end and all the fruit trees had severe problems with scab and virus. After I presented my plans to make sense of this, the owner told me that financial problems meant they would have to leave.

OPPOSITE: The Walled Garden

It was then sold on and the very well-known garden designer Christopher Bradley-Hole was invited to create a contemporary garden for the new owner. After a few years this owner too left and it was quickly bought by another couple, who asked me back to re-create a quintessentially English garden, as the modern look didn't sit well with them – although they wanted to retain the stunning box parterre on the south-west side of the house, as well as the big blocks of yew that can be seen as one approaches the house up the drive, accentuating the façade so very effectively.

So back came the plans for altering the large Walled Garden and we spent a long time tweaking them to suit their needs and desires. The new owner decided to build a large conservatory at the bottom of the garden. This was to be an orchid house. He bought my plans and then gave them over to a contractor to implement. The house changed hands again, but finally along came Steve and Linda Garnett, Bighton's saviours, who have now been there for twenty years. They had always wanted this house, so they were quick to act when they discovered it was for sale. It is once again a really happy family home – one can almost see the house smiling again.

After two or three years, I think it was 2003, I had a letter from Linda wondering if I could ever go back to sort out one or two little problems. Of course I was delighted, as I have always loved this very special place. I have worked there ever since and only just yesterday was ordering plants for a new project. This garden has been a joy from start to finish. I have had total support and encouragement from Steve and Linda, for which I am eternally grateful. They have honestly been the most

wonderful clients: their enthusiasm and positivity is gold dust for a designer and together we have worked on the entire garden.

We started once more with the Walled Garden. There were various problems that needed sorting, particularly with the setting out and the installation of the drainage (a problem which meant that plants had never thrived). There are two main entrances to this garden from the house and the paths run up two-thirds of the way to where ornamental gates in a yew hedge lead you into the top third of the garden.

However, my plans were focused on the beautiful conservatory, which was a central feature of the middle section of the garden. This area is divided by a wide grass path, either side of which are two square beds which we call the 'ripple beds' and which have to look good all year round. Within the beds is a combination of santolina, hebe, heuchera and *Helichrysum italicum*.

The path leads on to four rose beds circling a central pool with a fountain, before you get to two more ripple beds. Two wisteria tunnels run across the garden, dividing four quadrant beds generously planted in a more informal style.

On both sides of the conservatory (now known as the Pool House) are winter and spring beds. Behind the front façade are two gravel courtyards and these are planted with squares of pleached hornbeam and large Versailles caisses of topiary.

OPPOSITE: The ripple beds, planted for all-year-round interest
BELOW: The wisteria tunnel and central fountain

There are two generous borders running up the left and right sides of this middle section of the garden – the left side is given over to the vegetables, edged with stepover apples and fruit cages. On the right side is a box parterre set in gravel with a multi-stemmed *Betula utilis* subsp. *jacquemontii* in the middle of each bed.

OPPOSITE, CLOCKWISE FROM TOP LEFT: Wirework buttresses; stepover apples; the quadrant beds
BELOW: A close-up of one of the quadrant beds. In the background, a seat by George Carter.

This left the top end of the Walled Garden. I thought a plain green space would be good and Linda was keen to have this as a play area for the children, but she wanted a generous herbaceous border at the top. (There is also a charming bothy in the top left corner.)

It was important to have a focal point which would be visible from the Pool House. I am no architect, but my very gifted fellow garden designer George Carter came over one day and sketched a beautiful pavilion (in about twenty minutes – which mightily impressed Linda). He has continued to work for her, making several stunning small and significant buildings within the garden. At either end of this area there are now two iron pavilions that George and I thought would enhance the space, and on seeing the clock tower above the old stable yard,

we decided to echo the shape on the pavilions. I planted hornbeam up them to create two little secret seating places flanked by hornbeam mopheads. Herbs grow in small beds on the south-facing border and box balls are scattered about on the north-facing side.

I always think the approach to a house is important and so the drive was realigned, retaining the turning circle of grass and creating an avenue of *Tilia* x *europaea* 'Pallida' leading away from the house. Making a focal point at the end of this avenue are two hornbeam columns and a semicircular yew hedge left over from a Chelsea garden I had recently designed. A decorative urn sits in the centre.

The house is very classic in its simplicity and I didn't want to disturb this by fussy planting around it, so I created a curved two-tier box hedge following the line of the drive, backed by standard mop-headed hornbeam trees. These look fabulous lit up at night. Stone balls herald the entrance and exit.

There is a courtyard at the back of the house which separates the old stable yard from the house. This is where the family arrive and park their cars. So, to give privacy and soften this area, I put in a hornbeam hedge on stilts against the hard curved wall, with a solid choisya hedge facing the entrance and large yew topiary in planters. A stunning *Cornus controversa* sits in the middle. Following the drive on the outside of the Walled Garden is a line of *Pyrus calleriana* 'Chanticleer', underplanted with nepeta, taking you up to the old stable yard.

On the left of this drive is the orchard, now extensively planted with cherries and apples. George Carter was

commissioned to build an apple store, which sits enchantingly in the middle.

On the other side of the Walled Garden was an old Victorian sunken garden with boggy plants at the bottom of it. It had been severely fenced off by the previous owners. Linda expressed an interest in enlarging this body of water and it is now a large Decorative Pool with a bridge over it and planted with marginal and moisture-loving plants. George was commissioned to design another pavilion here, in memory of Linda's and Steve's mothers, and it is a stunning building. Inside there is

OPPOSITE: The avenue of *Tilia* x *europaea* 'Pallida' leading away from the house

ABOVE: Looking out through the gateway of the Walled Garden to the Decorative Pool
BELOW: Hornbeam mopheads and two-tier box shelving at the entrance to the house

LEFT: The new Orangery Garden
BELOW: The gravelled area of the Orangery Garden
OPPOSITE: The planted terrace with the furniture I designed for Linda

beautiful leadwork by Brian Turner depicting some of the mothers' favourite flowers. Masses of magnolias now grow around it, as well as river birch. It is so lovely to have areas of different character and when you have the luck to have a large garden, you can really make use of this. Coming out of the side entrance of the Walled Garden, one sees a powerful jet of water shooting up from the middle of the pool. On the far side large *Dicksonia antarctica*, with other ferns, look stunningly dramatic.

The last big project was the Orangery Garden. This terraced area is for entertaining and I had some garden furniture made for Linda. This led, ultimately, to my designing the range of garden furniture called the Helmingham Collection (see page 168).

Pleached *Betula utilis* subsp. *jacquemontii* trees divide this terrace surrounded by flower beds from a contemporary space with a David Harber sculpture in the centre and featuring box balls in gravel and different varieties of grasses. *Prunus fruticosa* 'Globosa' mopheads give it vertical interest and a yew parterre leads on to a fabulous greenhouse, now filled with exotic treasures. The gravel path outside this garden was interspersed with diamonds of brick and the whole length is spiked by half-standards of *Prunus lusitanica* underplanted by nepeta which flows out, softening the edge. Box balls punctuate this soft planting.

To me, the house and garden seem to relish the attention they are getting. (Steve and Linda, with Philip Hooper's help, have also completely redecorated and embellished the house.) We are still thinking about ways to further enhance the garden and I really look forward to my fun and inspiring trips to magical Bighton and working with the marvellous garden team.

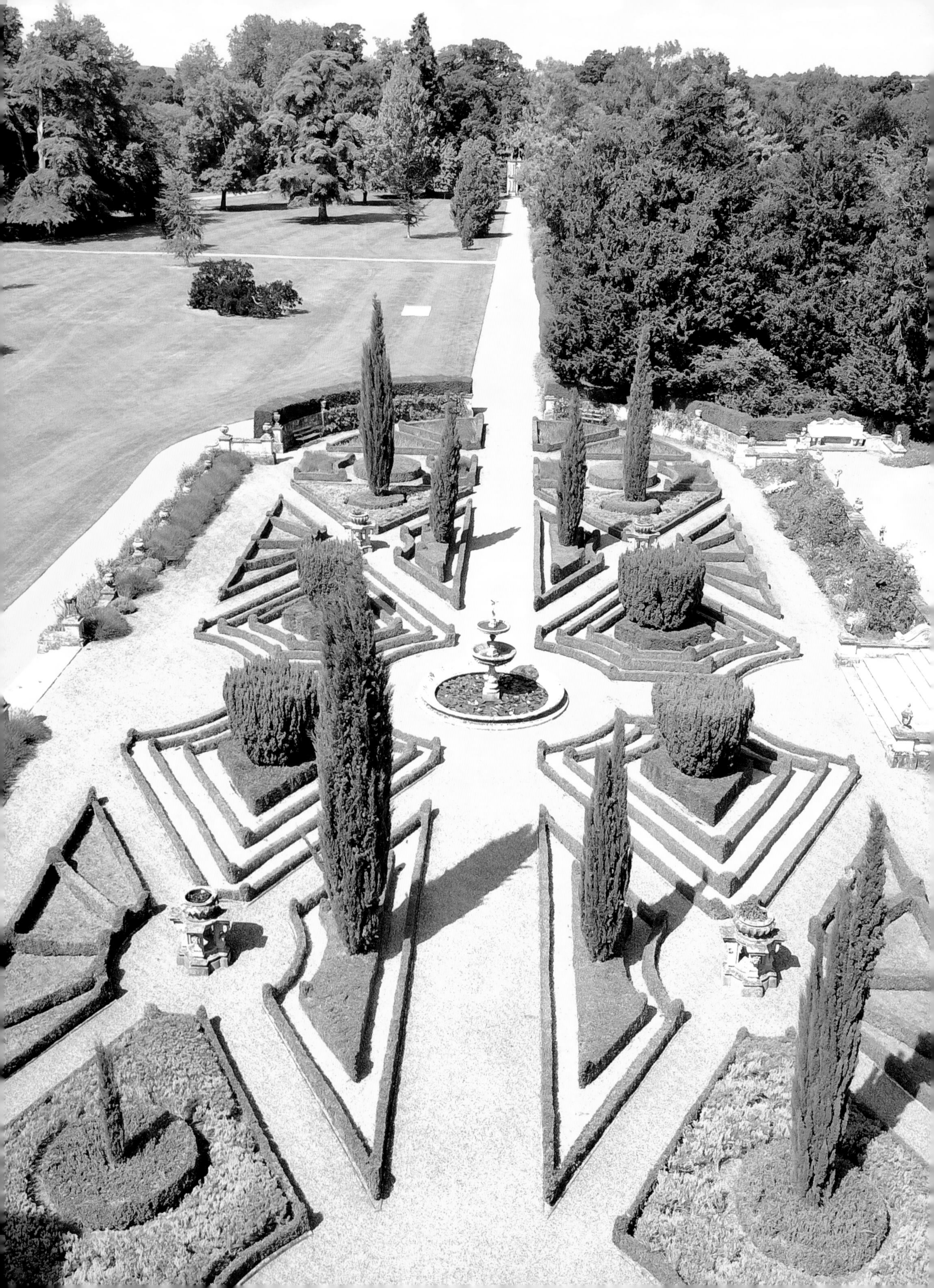

WILTON HOUSE

WILTSHIRE

ABOVE: Looking towards the Orangery

This magnificent house has been in the family of the Earls of Pembroke for more than four and a half centuries. It sits on the site of a priory founded in the ninth century. After the Dissolution of the Monasteries Henry VIII presented the house and estate to one of his favourites (and one of the most powerful men of the day), William Herbert, 1st Earl of Pembroke.

The gift was made in 1544 and soon after that William Herbert began work on a large Tudor house set round a central courtyard. It has long been claimed that the Tudor house was designed by Hans Holbein the Younger. As Holbein died in 1543 this seems unlikely. However, two parts of the house, the Holbein Porch and the Holbein Arch, still bear his name.

Because of damage resulting from civil wars and a serious fire, the house was partly rebuilt in 1653 by Inigo Jones; it was later modernized by James Wyatt in 1801.

The extensive gardens have also undergone many changes, the most outstanding feature being the Palladian bridge built in 1736 by the 7th Earl,

OPPOSITE: The Italian Garden

the 'Architect Earl' as he came to be known, who exerted great influence over the grounds, naturalizing the formality.

THE CLOISTER GARDEN

When, in 1997, as one of my first jobs, I was asked by the 17th Earl of Pembroke to 'do something' with a very dank and depressing courtyard surrounded by cloisters, I found the prospect rather daunting.

This courtyard was surely designed to be looked down on from the surrounding upper cloisters. It was important not to distract from the wealth of pictures, furniture and sculptures that were housed within these cloisters, and yet any garden would need to have the strength and elegance to match up to the ornate architecture. In an account of Wilton dated 1623 there was a description of a knot garden. I took this as my inspiration for what is now called the Cloister Garden.

By luck, in the centre of the courtyard there was a seventh-century Venetian wellhead. The outward-facing sides of this wellhead all had different patterns on them and I chose four which could make up the knot garden and not be too dominant. I used very few plants here: box bushes make up the knots, with a standard bay in the centre of each bed. Cotton lavender goes around the outside. A plain whitish brick in herringbone pattern shows up the garden well against the dark walls of the house.

When William, the present (18th) Earl, arrived in 2012, he found a wealth of treasures lying around the garden, old sculptures and other artefacts, and he got a specialist in to value some of these incredible finds. When the specialist saw the Venetian wellhead in the centre of the Cloister Garden, he was amazed to see this

priceless antique outside and suggested that William really ought to preserve it by taking it into the Gallery. William told him that he couldn't possibly remove it from the garden, that it was important there (and what would I say?), but sense prevailed and, to satisfy everyone, he had a copy made for the garden. (I was totally unaware of this until he told me much later!)

THE ITALIAN GARDEN

The unsung heroine of Wilton is Catherine Woronzow, the daughter of an early-nineteenth-century Russian ambassador to Britain. She married the 11th Earl in 1808 and from all accounts she was remarkable in her work inside the house. It is thanks to her that Wilton

OPPOSITE: The Cloister Garden
RIGHT: A detail of one of the beds, beside the Venetian wellhead

combines the charm of an English country house with the splendour of a continental palace. In 1820, with the sculptor Richard Westmacott, she also designed an Italian Garden and a loggia and orangery on the west side of the house, and rebuilt the Holbein Arch. And with her son Sidney she paid for the new Italian Romanesque basilica of the Church of St Mary and St Nicholas in the town of Wilton, which was erected in 1840.

Over the years the Italian Garden was changed to a sunken garden, then in the 1970s Henry Pembroke tried a rose garden; but the roses just didn't like it, and the garden looked pretty tired. In 2006, William's mother, Claire, asked me to do a new design for this garden that she could give him for Christmas. I felt it should be taken back to the Italian Garden that Catherine Pembroke had put in back in the nineteenth century.

We had all the original bed shapes and a decorative central pool and indeed some sketches, so it wasn't too difficult to re-create this garden but in a more contemporary fashion. Josephine Marston did an electrifying and beautiful watercolour of my design, which Claire then gave her son for his Christmas present – so I just had to make it come true!

THE ITALIAN GARDEN

Now the Italian Garden is established, it stands up well against the imposing house. The beautiful orangery at the northern side of the garden is aligned on the circular pool in the middle. A huge terrace and generous steps take you down to the level of the garden, passing by large borders. The main axis of the garden leads out of the house from big French windows in the library. The view of the Holbein Arch beyond is splendid. The borders now have box-edged beds in them, with corresponding beds on either side of the central path. These beds all have different geometric designs within them and some are filled with low-growing *Santolina chamaecyparissus* and *Saxifraga* x *urbium*. Eight Italian cypress give vertical interest and four large goblet-shaped yews flank the pool. Since then, I have worked with the family to create a Family Garden with a tennis court and summer house and I did some new planting in the Forecourt, refreshing the original planting. We planted many climbing roses up the walls to soften this quite severe building: 'Climbing Étoile de Hollande', Claire

Austin, Wollerton Old Hall, James Galway, The Generous Gardener, Mortimer Sackler, Shropshire Lad, Gertrude Jekyll, Scepter'd Isle and Strawberry Hill now clothe the walls.

It is wonderful to have the enthusiasm and positivity of the present generation, who are making such a success of this historic property.

OPPOSITE: Watercolour by Josephine Marston, 2006, showing Wilton House and my design for the Italian Garden
ABOVE: The realized Italian Garden

ALDEBURGH

SUFFOLK

ABOVE: Bumblebee on white allium

This house is in the middle of Aldeburgh, a town which is, of course, a major tourist attraction, very well known for its association with Benjamin Britten and the Aldeburgh Festival. The shingle beach is also a great draw. The owner knew Chris McDaniel, a hugely skilled contractor, and it was through his recommendation that she invited me over.

She was very apologetic when she rang me and suggested I wouldn't like anything to do with this garden. This was immediately challenging to me and I asked her why not? But when I got to the house, I realized just what a challenge it presented. I could understand why she questioned me.

The house was to have a thorough restorartion, including having certain parts pulled down and rebuilt. The garden was separated into three areas by retaining walls 3–4.25 metres/10–14 feet high.

She asked me whether I had ever done such a garden and I had to admit that I hadn't. As I looked out over the roofs of the town houses with a glimpse of the cold North Sea, I saw a horizon which I had never experienced before. Trying to come up with a compliment, I told her it had a feeling of Florence – which she found rather hilarious. She remarked that perhaps Florence didn't have howling north winds to cope with – and our view was not of church spires, but on to the roof of a restaurant.

OPPOSITE: The view from the house

We decided where she wanted a flat lawn, and where the kitchen garden should be, and the main entertainment area, and I did some sketches.

The first thing the contractor had to do was pull down the high walls, which were definitely not possible to work with. Interestingly enough, no sooner had he embarked on this than he rang me to suggest I should come over. When I arrived, he told me that the walls had no footings and they were sitting on jelly. 'Jelly?', I asked. There were numerous springs that popped up all over the garden which made building anything high impossible . . . So, how to redesign this whole garden?

I did have a major designer's block at that moment. It was Chris, the contractor, who remarked that he had once made a garden with terraces 1 metre/39 inches high; he thought that might work here, with the changes of level.

The clever architect who was working on the house restoration agreed that he would draw up a plan with the level changes (in those days, I felt quite incapable of doing this correctly). He also suggested that maybe we could capture the water from the springs and have some sort of rill coming down into a pool at the bottom. The springs alone would not provide enough water to feed a decorative water feature, so we agreed to put in a pump to circulate the captured water from the pool. That way

LEFT: The view up to the house from the bottom pool, showing the terraces
ABOVE: How it was!

we could have three spouts, with only one using the spring water.

A newly built generous terrace with a corner of herbs leads out of the house, and raised beds are planted with climbing roses and lavender and other perennials.

The first level is a plain lawn flanked by two parterres: one with a diamond pattern of box hedging studded with box balls, *Iris* 'Sable' and Kent roses; in the other lavender and *Miscanthus sinensis* 'Morning Light' are planted, punctuated by standard *Pyrus salicifolia*.

A secluded garden beneath the house terrace is protected by an osier fence. Here the owner can sit and read, protected from the wind and the noise of the town.

Steps lead down to the next level, where we have herbaceous borders with a winding path running through, a crab apple tree and Hybrid Musk roses at one end. On the level beneath this we planted formal clipped bushes of skimmia, santolina, sarcococca and pittosporum. In the middle is the cistern with its spouts of water. To one side is a seating area with pleached birch trees. The kitchen garden, with a new cedar greenhouse, is on the other. Raised beds of oak grow varied and plentiful vegetables and fruit.

The bottom level is a gravel space with a deep border with shrubs such as carpenteria, hydrangea, buddleia and daphne, and tall-growing perennials against the wall at the end of the garden. Then there is a path that leads you down to the main street. This path has trees and shrubs on either side to make a very green alley; and at the bottom a highly decorative door gives you entry on to the street.

Leading round the house from the main kitchen terrace, there is a herb garden on the corner and, opposite, a collection of Rugosa roses. To the front of the house, in a space sheltered by a new wall off the roadside, we planted scented roses and created a small sitting area. And all along the front of the house is a

OPPOSITE: An aerial view showing the finished garden
RIGHT: The pool on the bottom terrace
BELOW: Capturing the water

LEFT: Steps lead from the sunken garden on the lowest level up to the vegetable garden
BELOW: The lowest terrace
OPPOSITE, ABOVE: *Salvia nemorosa* 'Caradonna' and white alliums in the sunken garden
OPPOSITE, BELOW: The green path to the High Street

new garden, with trees and dividing hedges, shrubs and perennials.

Florence it is not, but despite all the problems it turned out well – though, goodness, not without a great deal of stress! Mercifully, the client retained her sense of humour and kept calm in all the various adventures of creating the garden. It really had settled in when I saw it last, and looked beautiful. The gardener has surpassed himself in maintaining and improving the garden, which still has constant challenges.

BELL HOUSE

SUFFOLK

ABOVE: The jets!

Bell House is in the middle of the village of Denston. Even though there was an existing cottage here, it ended up by being not just a restoration but almost a new build.

The client had previously lived in the big house over the fields. When her husband died she decided to move to a smaller property but still in the area she loved, where she could continue to enjoy the view over the park. I had helped her considerably at the big house, and she very kindly asked me back to design her new garden.

I imagined that she would want a low-maintenance garden, but thankfully not. She wanted a garden which everyone would admire and enjoy. Having had a large garden which was beautifully maintained by skilled staff, in this new garden she wanted to be hands-on. It was a long job with many problems with both the house and the garden and with some very difficult weather situations. This was made possible by the hard work and efficiency of Johnny Winter and his team, who worked incredibly hard under very challenging circumstances.

OPPOSITE: The parterre, planted with *Prunus lusitanica* and nepeta

We started on the plans in 2014. First, we had to take the hard decision to remove some trees. There was a row of Leylandii conifers; taking them down presented no problems or heartache. But there were also some once-beautiful trees which were in poor condition and a few which would cast too much shade over the garden. The fate of an old shed and a double row of apple and pear trees had to be considered. The shed had to go, but we decided to keep the fruit trees, reducing and retaining the best in a staggered row, and use them within a fresh design.

I always think that the first impression is important, and how I deal with the approach to a house is high on my radar. We made a new entrance and driveway and the main garden was hidden from it by the house. A simple – but very pleasing – approach was created, basically a grass lawn planted with spring bulbs, with different trees on either side. A long field maple hedge dictated the boundary and also provided privacy.

The side entrance – where most people arrive, as it is closest to the parking area – was densely planted with evergreens and fragrant plants that could cope with an east-facing wall. These include abelia, artemisia, cistus, perovskia, hebe, roses, lavender, and buckets of tulips and hyacinths. Borders surround the house on every side and on every aspect climbing plants clothe the walls. We had, of course, to bear in mind how much light they would get and plant accordingly.

The north border is on either side of the formal front door, from where a path leads you to the road. Hence it has both to look good all year and also to tolerate shade. Ferns, hellebores, viburnums, bergenias, foxgloves, anemones and euphorbia, planted with early tulips and daffodils, achieve this. Here again it was very important to create privacy, so we planted a high hornbeam hedge.

We planned a generous terrace, leading out from the house facing south. Here is the main garden, where quadrant beds surround a circular bed with a fountain.

OPPOSITE: Bell House, newly restored and all in place
RIGHT: The box-edged circular bed surrounding the fountain
BELOW: Planting in the quadrant beds, including *Penstemon* 'Apple Blossom' and *Lysimachia clethroides*

The centrepiece here is planted with broken box hedging and in the middle jets of water, set in stone, shoot up to different heights. This was all meticulously designed by Roger Orford of Miles Waterscapes.

The client stressed that she wanted the beds to be flowering from midsummer onwards, the spring colour to be created with masses of bulbs. This is a sensible idea when space is limited. Roses and herbaceous plants such as peonies, anthemis, veronicas, campanulas, scabious, bergenias and iris make up the early summer display, with repeat-flowering roses, heleniums, asters, lysimachia, verbena and penstemons keeping the colour going till the frosts come. This garden is flanked on either side by what we called the palisade of trees – *Amelanchier* x *grandiflora* 'Robin Hill' underplanted with nepeta – creating privacy as well as an effective framework for the garden.

On the west side is a different form of a parterre: this runs down the length of the house, with squares edged with *Osmanthus* x *burkwoodii* clipped low, infilled alternately with santolina and nepeta, each with a half-standard Portugal laurel in the centre.

This balances the height and strength of the house, working together with borders on either side of a path and ending with a big square of lavender among which stand obelisks of climbing roses surrounding a circular space with a side entrance to the terrace. This gives the area some 'body'. With the evergreen element and the summer flowers, it provides interest all through the year (as well as access).

On this side of the house is the lawn, with a lovely sculpture which my client had shipped over from her estate in Chile. Beyond this is the new Woodland Garden, incorporating the fruit trees which we had kept and grass paths wrapping round these, creating large beds which have now been densely planted with woodland plants and lovely trees. Large, semi-mature magnolias, lilacs, betulas, nothofagus, cornus, acers

OPPOSITE: The parterre, each bed planted with a central standard of *Prunus lusitanica* surrounded by catmint and cotton lavender; beyond, a palisade of *Amelanchier* 'Robin Hill'
RIGHT: On the lawn, the sculpture that my client shipped from Chile
BELOW: A view from the terrace, across the lawn to the Woodland Garden. The pale orange roses in the foreground of the photograph are Sweet Dreams, the climbers behind are The Generous Gardener and Open Arms.

and sorbus, underplanted with shrubs and perennials, now make this garden look as though it has been here for fifty years.

Designing a garden from scratch presents a rare opportunity, and a blank canvas gets my imagination going overtime. Coupled with a generous, enthusiastic and knowledgeable owner, this made it a smashing job to do. Sitting on the terrace with everything bursting with form, structure and colour and gazing over green and luscious parkland isn't a bad occupation! I might add, to go back after four years and find it immaculately kept, with the plants that proved either too weak or too invasive moved to other places, gave huge pleasure and reward. As it would to any designer.

BELOW: In the Woodland Garden, *Allium stipitatum* 'Mount Everest', with *Betula utilis* subsp. *jacquemontii*, a purple-leaved ligularia and grasses
OPPOSITE, ABOVE LEFT: *Stipa tenuissima*
OPPOSITE, ABOVE RIGHT: *Heuchera villosa* 'Palace Purple'
OPPOSITE, BELOW: The winding path through the Woodland Garden

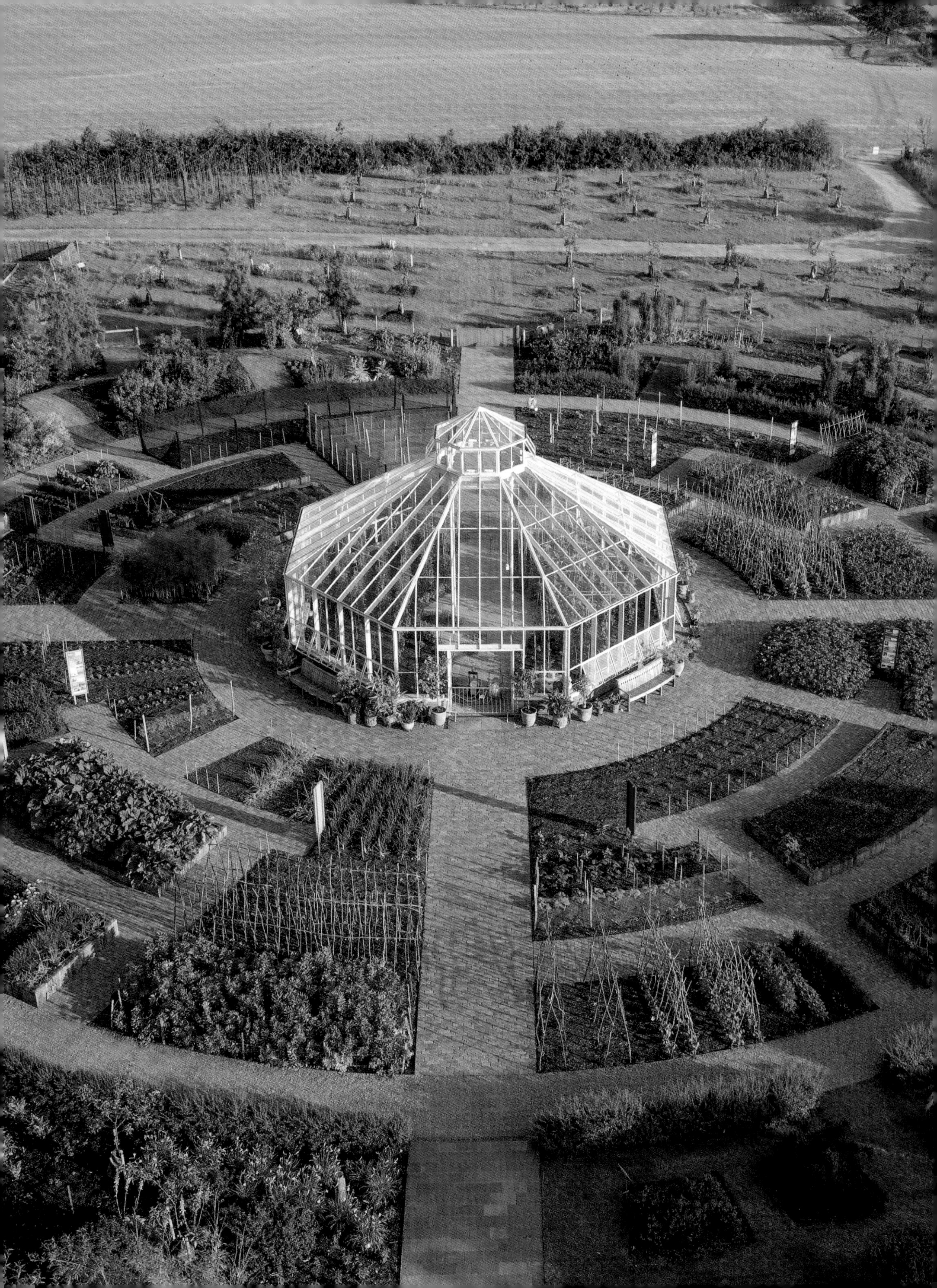

RHS HYDE HALL

ESSEX

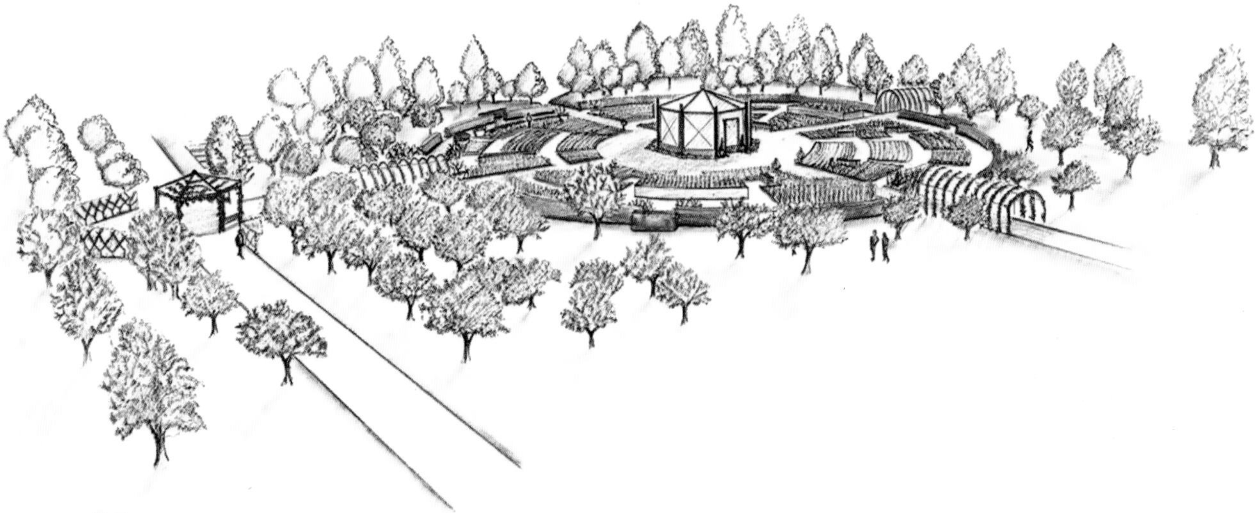

ABOVE: Drawing by Jane Bailey of my plan for the Global Growth Vegetable Garden

THE GLOBAL GROWTH VEGETABLE GARDEN

In 2010 the Royal Horticultural Society asked me to be one of their garden advisers. Each of the RHS gardens has its own team, led by the on-site manager and a curator, but independent garden advisers are assigned to each of the five gardens, mainly to support and encourage, sometimes to suggest – and, if possible, *never* to criticize!

At one of our meetings, it was suggested that Hyde Hall should have a proper vegetable garden, like the other RHS gardens. So far it had merely had allotments, which, however popular, didn't illustrate the art of growing vegetables and fruit. I said, rather flippantly, that I would design them a kitchen garden and, before long, I had been accepted to do this on a professional basis.

I thought seriously about Hyde Hall and where it is situated. My train of thought culminated in the Global Growth Vegetable Garden.

OPPOSITE: The garden in its glory, 2017

The estate at Hyde Hall was purchased by Dick and Helen Robinson in 1955. It is six miles from Chelmsford, only thirty minutes by train from London, and yet it is set in a landscape of rolling hills and panoramic views.

The Robinsons farmed the land and became increasingly interested in making a garden. It had heavy clay soil, few trees and was exposed to the elements as it sat on top of a hill. By 1963 they had embarked on planting shelter belts and when they were given rhododendron seedlings they planted them to form the beginnings of the Woodland Garden. They became avid gardeners and created the Hilltop Garden with island beds of shrubs and perennials. As they became older, they realized they could not continue farming, and nor could they look after the garden as they would like.

In 1993 they gave the garden and estate to the RHS and the first masterplan was drawn up for the site by landscape designers Colvin and Moggridge. Today the estate encompasses 148 hectares/365 acres, of which 36 hectares/90 acres are leased to a tenant farmer and 34 hectares/85 acres are grassland.

In 2001 the Dry Garden was created. It was one of the first large-scale landscapes undertaken here by the RHS and it was further enlarged a decade later. It is now home to more than five hundred different species of plants.

In 2012 I started to think about how I would create a new and exciting vegetable garden. I was shown the plot, which was the home of several polytunnels and a general waste dump for anything not being used.

OPPOSITE: Old polytunnels where the new garden is going to go
RIGHT: Work starting in 2016

The space was 50 metres/164 feet in diameter and was at the bottom of the sloping formal rose garden and herbaceous borders, divided from them by a high hornbeam hedge.

Beyond the boundary is the natural rolling landscape and it was important to link the formal with the countryside and also to embrace the very distinctive undulating Dry Garden which sits next door. There needed to be a major focal point as you leave the farmhouse and walk through the Rose Garden. It had to be a serious destination.

How could I make this garden different, interesting and educational? As it was so close to London, I wanted to attract a different audience to my garden; most of all I wanted children to learn about food and how it is grown and how it reaches the table. At that time, there was little or no education in the inner cities about where our food comes from.

The more I explored this idea the more I learned about what different plants different parts of the world eat. I was amazed, for example, to find out that Asians eat plants that we merely know as decorative flowers for our gardens.

The global idea started to form and with that and the forthcoming London Olympics, I decided that the kitchen garden should reflect the globe and therefore be round. It should then be subdivided into quarters to showcase plants of different origin: Europe and the Middle East; North and Central America; South America; and Asia.

I had my wonderful assistant Jane Bailey to help me and she researched all the plants that we could grow in this climate that yet were not used in a culinary way in this country. Fabio Nalin did some amazing visuals all the way through our journey.

We finalized the plans with a dream of putting an octagonal glasshouse in the middle. This was to be very large, to be seen from the farmhouse, and light in structure so that the landscape beyond could be glimpsed through it.

We had to present our plans to the Planning Committee, which was pretty terrifying. As a back-up I had thought that, if the budget didn't stretch to a vast greenhouse, we could put a large fruit cage in the middle. The President at that time was the famous land-scape architect and garden designer Elizabeth Banks.

After we had finished the presentation she asked me what I wanted in the middle. I said, 'Of course a greenhouse!' 'Well,' she responded, 'have it then.'

The plan was developed and construction began in 2016. Curved beds of different shapes and contrasting heights were surrounded by metal-edged Italian porphyry stone paths. This circular area was planted with an osmanthus hedge, and mounds were created in each of the four corners with trees and shrubs appropriate to the continent below them in the beds.

The creation of the Global Growth Vegetable Garden was supported by Witan Investment Trust and it is an educational space. The greenhouse, which was given at cost by Hartley Botanic, houses the less hardy edible crops. Throughout the garden traditional varieties are being grown alongside exciting new plants which are not generally associated with food in the UK. On a recent visit I was told that every plant in the garden is edible in some form, even the osmanthus hedge flowers, which the Japanese use to make tea.

Matt Oliver is the young horticulturist who is the main inspiration behind all the varieties grown here. Some of the rare and obscure plants that are grown are listed in the box to the right.

Dahlias, hostas, ferns and many Asian spice plants are all grown successfully and many are taken by the chef to add variety to the menus.

This interesting garden fulfils all the criteria that it was designed for. First and foremost, to show visitors the extraordinary range of plants grown around the world – many of them unknown in Britain.

It is very near the east end of London, where there are huge numbers of schoolchildren who live in the city and rarely, if ever, come out to the country. They learn, perhaps, even about foods in the country of their origin.

Lastly, it is a lovely garden to walk around and I hope it gives pleasure and interest to all the thousands of visitors who come to Hyde Hall each year.

OPPOSITE: A drone picture showing the four continents radiating from the central greenhouse
BELOW: Fitting in comfortably with the rest of the garden

EUROPE

Brassica oleracea (Botrytis Group) 'Asparagoides' (nine-star cauliflower); *Cyperus esculentus* var. *sativus* (tiger nut)

ASIA

Basella alba (Malabar spinach); *Vigna unguiculata* subsp. *sesquipedalis* (asparagus bean, yardlong bean)

NORTH AND CENTRAL AMERICA

Apios americana (potato bean); *Solanum retroflexum* (wonderberry)

SOUTH AMERICA

Smallanthus sonchifolius (yacon); *Solanum sisymbriifolium* (vila-vila); *Ullucus tuberosus* (one of the most widely eaten Andean tuber plants)

STONE HOUSE

SUFFOLK

ABOVE: An aerial view – incuding the North Sea

In 2018 my son-in-law and my daughter bought a house in Southwold, an attractive seaside town built on a low hill which has been eroded by the sea to form cliffs and sandy beaches. James had been brought up there, as his father, a doctor, came into the local practice when the family were all very young.

James and Selina have their family home near Bury St Edmunds and in 2018 an opportunity came up to buy this wonderful house in Southwold – and with it came a grass tennis court, something James's father had always hankered after!

It is a pretty grey stone house perched on Gun Hill, very close to the golden sands and the North Sea. There was a fort here which had its origins in the Southwold defences constructed in 1588. The house was built around 1807 but has had further additions at different times.

I had not designed a seaside garden before and I realized it would be quite a challenge. I knew that most plants would not enjoy being blasted by the salt-laden winds that blew up from the beach, and the front garden, facing the

OPPOSITE: The new double borders, with *Leucanthemum* x *superbum* 'Becky' in the foreground

LEFT: Pink valerian and purple sedum flowering in the border in late summer
BELOW: The top lawn, with raised bed and double borders
OPPOSITE: Tulips in the spring

sea, was right in line for this. However, at the back of the house was a large walled garden on a steep slope more or less protected from the elements. It was charming, and I rather fell in love with it. I told Selina and James that I didn't want to spoil the whimsical atmosphere. On the other hand, it had to be a useable garden that could be enjoyed by their family and friends.

There was a great deal to restore in the house and it was covered in scaffolding for over a year – which had its drawbacks for me, as at the same time I was trying to design the garden.

The garden walls all had to be repointed and in some places they needed complete rebuilding. The paths were redesigned and the crazy paving was replaced by superb York stone. In order to achieve the required privacy, as well as protection from the ferocious winds, we created more height by erecting a woven osier fence rising above the walls, and then planted thirty-four pleached hornbeams with the right stem length to disguise the fence.

We had to design the approach off Gun Hill and the front borders, but the main work was within the walls behind the house. In order to make the garden work, we terraced it. On the top terrace, there is against the wall a raised bed thickly planted with roses and perennials, and then a plain grass lawn with a huge sycamore tree. A retaining wall divides this area from two double herbaceous borders that lead from the house to the back of the garden, where steps take one to the middle terrace. These generous borders are planted with perennials, punctuated by pittosporum balls, and roses are planted at the back of the borders against the low retaining wall. A mass of tulips and alliums gives a fabulous show before the main performance kicks in.

Already existing holm oaks (*Quercus ilex*) provide the shade at the end of these borders and have, over the years, become well adjusted to the climate. A hedge of salt-resistant *Griselinia littoralis* is planted at the back of the right-hand border, and then the ground slopes down to another retaining wall before reaching the bottom level. This steep slope has been planted with a wildflower mat and has a wonderful collection of natural flora throughout the growing season.

At the bottom is an informal lawn with two huge holm oaks and we have planted more trees for privacy. This area leads you to the grass tennis court, at the back of which are steps to a higher level. Here we planted two big rose borders (the roses cascade down, breaking up the high wall) and made a seating area which allows you to view the fierce tennis matches that take place over the year. I told James that I wouldn't have anything to do with the rebuild of the court. I just know what a tricky business it is, and indeed in the end it was taking the gardener half his time to look after it. (Now they have asked a turf expert at the local golf course to take it on, which has relieved the gardener.)

The new kitchen terrace is a large space looking out over the marshlands and cattle grazing pastures and over to Walberswick across the Blyth estuary. Flocks of geese and murmurations of starlings are a wonder to see at the right time of the year and day. I have planted big pots with seasonal plants which, with two plantings, last from May to November. James and Selina had seen and loved lavender-edged steps at a friend's house, so we planned generous steps to lead out from this new terrace to the bottom of the Walled Garden. I have

BELOW: The raised rose terrace at the back of the tennis court
OPPOSITE: Lavender 'Grosso' lining steps to the lower garden

LEFT: *Erigeron karvinskianus* self-seeding at the back of the terrace
BELOW: *Rosa* The Mill on the Floss
OPPOSITE: *Lilium regale* 'Album' with *Nepeta* x *faassenii* 'Kit Cat' in the raised border at the side of the top lawn

planted staggered rows of 'Grosso' lavender to give a purple haze on either side of the steps.

As you approach the house across Gun Hill, there is a low wall before going through the entrance and arrival at the house, so I planted a row of clipped holm oaks in a narrow border. For the first year these looked pretty miserable, blasted by the winds and suffering from not being watered enough. But I was fairly confident that they should establish themselves, as there were similar holm oaks nearby. Luckily, with tender loving care they have survived, along with big box balls and latterly a hedge of lavender 'Hidcote' and pompons of alliums. Against the front of the house is a box shelf with raised domes within it. Simple, structured planting.

Through a gate at the side of the house one arrives on a lawn looking straight out to sea (over a famous row of brightly coloured beach huts). I have planted borders at either end of this lawn, being doubly careful to plant strong, salt-resistant plants. These include Rugosa roses, tough grasses such as elymus and festuca, elaeagnus, fuchsia, bupleurum, escallonia, centranthus, sedum and phlomis. Every year annuals are planted to add to the colour and seaside flavour.

It was such a great opportunity to do a garden from absolute scratch, albeit in challenging circumstances. I had total support from James and Selina and enormous help from their team of contractors, who couldn't have been better or more proactive. My assistant Jane Bailey was instrumental in making it all happen.

FRAMSDEN HALL

SUFFOLK

ABOVE: Framsden Hall in the Suffolk countryside

Framsden Hall was built in 1485 and came into the Tollemache family early in the 1500s. When Tim and I got engaged in 1969, we were shown three houses on the estate which were possible for us to live in. Tim didn't want me to be influenced by him, so he didn't tell me which one he liked most.

Once I had seen around the house, I found it entrancing – as well as being very impressed by its great age and historical importance. So, aged nearly twenty, I announced rather precociously that I felt Framsden was by far the most special and nicest of the choices. Luckily Tim felt the same, and so we set about thinking what we could do with it to restore it into our family home. We were thinking that we would be there for fifteen years at least.

The house has a moat which leads off the north-east side of the house and encircles a garden within on three sides. We had to dredge it, and we hired a digger to remove nearly five hundred years of silt. Tim has three brothers and they all came over to cart away some of the removable debris. We had great fun lighting bonfires and getting stuck in mud.

OPPOSITE: The new Lavender Garden within the moat

The interior of the house needed a lot of work, and our potential drawing room was a chicken shed. However, undeterred (and with the help of an architect), we designed the house and decided how the rooms would work.

Originally there would have been no floors or ceilings, just a big central hall. This space showed the most marvellous carved beams at the top, with queen posts, cusped braces and medieval carvings of faces, angels and floral decorations. The only room which had a ceiling was the 'chicken shed', which had been the solar, where the master of the house would have lived with his family. Above this was the main bedroom. Both of these rooms had wonderful beams and carved faces on brackets. We had to repair the ceiling, and though we managed to retain some of the brackets and masks, we couldn't save the beams, so we had to have modern ones made and distressed to look aged.

The entire façade of the house had to be removed so the rendering could be replaced – this made the ancient building look like an upside-down boat. However, we repaired the damage, replaced the render and employed someone skilled at pargetting. This is a decorative practice using stencils and other tools which makes patterns on the render: it has to be done while the plaster panels are still wet. Pargetting has been used on old houses throughout East Anglia (beautiful examples can be seen at Lavenham, for instance).

However, I have to admit that my decoration of the house was on the whole pretty disastrous. Such is the impulsive nature of youth. I was trying so hard to impress that, inexperienced as I was, I did not take stock of the character of the house. I certainly had not had any practice at decorating historic houses – I can only be thankful that I wasn't let loose on Helmingham at that time!

The house took over eighteen months to fully restore, and while the work was going on we rented a cottage nearby. I used to come over and spend hours scraping the limewash off the magnificent carved fifteenth-century beams. (It is hard to imagine that those huge beams were once acorns – I suppose some time before 1066.) Anyway, we finally moved into half the house and lived for what seemed an interminable time among pipes, wires, dust and open floorboards. But at last we were finished. And I became pregnant.

* * *

There was a large misshapen lawn in front of the house, along with an old irreparable greenhouse and some areas of lawn and shrubs. Not having a clue how to go about sorting all this out, we hired Notcutts; the resident designer was Paul Miles, who came over to design the garden.

Yew hedges were put in around the sides of the moat for protection and privacy, and within we had rectangular beds of yellow roses (as I had rather grandly mentioned that I *only* liked yellow roses).

Paul designed us a front border of mainly shrubs, about which I knew nothing, so I wrote labels on them and learned them off by heart, from left to right. When anybody asked me what a particular shrub was, I had to recite the litany from the beginning of the border. At the back of the house Paul persuaded me to have a heather garden. Goodness knows why he thought that would be a good idea, and also why I allowed it in the heart of Suffolk. (Such is the impotence of ignorance.)

I came from a very keen riding family. My mother and all five of us children would go riding together. When I arrived in Suffolk I soon realized that it was not the best riding county, with ploughed fields going right up to the hedges and car and lorry drivers not fully understanding the dangers of riding a young horse along the lanes. We were, however, near Newmarket. So I decided that I would breed racehorses and sell on the foals. For the first five years I had an amazing time with four or five mares, successfully selling their foals. I adored going around the studs and choosing the stallions, and the heady experience of the sales at Tattersalls.

On 3 October 1973 our daughter, Selina, was born and she came home to a brand-new nursery and all the comforts of a first-born child. Two wonderful years ensued but then, in 1975, my father-in-law died and our lives changed. Tim had to take over the estate now, without his father to guide him, and so, with the agreement of my mother-in-law, we took the decision to move into Helmingham. Off we went for forty-two years – to return like homing pigeons in 2017.

We were lucky enough to have Tim's brother Michael, with his wife, Terrie, and their children move from London and make Framsden their very happy home for about twenty-five years. They made several changes to the house which further improved it and created a wonderful garden (having the foresight first to plant large trees for windbreaks). In particular, within the confines of the moat, Terrie made a beautiful rose garden specializing in historic roses. They also made a lovely herb garden outside the Summer Room (previously the old butter-making room).

They left the house when the children had grown up, and it was then let out to various tenants who proved sometimes great and sometimes not so great. One way or another, when we finally came back the garden was a wilderness.

Luckily the family arrangements of our move allowed enough time to do extensive work on Framsden and for my son and his family to create wonderful rooms for the children at Helmingham – the same ones that we did so long ago, which had gone through the stages of cots, then bunk beds, then single beds, then double beds and then back again to single beds. (The early years followed by the teenage years and then the young marrieds. And their children.)

At Framsden, we put in double glazing and replaced the old Crittal windows, opened up the partition wall between our new kitchen and the sitting room, and revealed the oldest part of the house, where there was some beautiful carving. I had continued to feel guilty about covering it up all those years ago, and when we revealed it again, it was like saying hello to an old friend.

So, once more, it became our much-loved home, a roundabout of a lifetime but this time suited to just us with our dogs, though always open to family, friends and especially (oh, joy!) grandchildren.

The house now has a different use. We have a large family room which serves as a dining room but also has sofas and a television. A toy box means the children can play about while we linger over a bottle.

The attic is a children's treasure trove, with all my old mini dresses and hats and fake jewellery, cars and Lego, and a lovely room at the end which is the art room where they can paint on the walls, doors and floors to their great enjoyment and fun. (No paints are allowed outside the door.)

The house is always welcoming and it is a place where we are very happy. Curiously the dogs only took two hours before settling in here. I think they appreciated always knowing where we were.

* * *

Framsden Hall – our home, old and new

OPPOSITE, ABOVE: The Tithe Barn, built in 1485
OPPOSITE, BELOW: Horses in the House Meadow
ABOVE: *Rosa* Lichfield Angel
RIGHT, ABOVE: *Dahlia* 'Verrone's Obsidian'
RIGHT, BELOW: *Thalictrum* Splendide White

Outside the house there is a spectacular barn - built at the same time as the house, and probably the largest tithe barn in the east of England. It is enormous and we restored the roof when we first came here in the early 1970s, which was a blessing, as now it is dry and safe. Every year we hold one or two charity events there (as well as a village barn dance, which is always great fun).

On the other side of the barn are the stables which Tim had built when I was breeding racehorses. They are let out but I have now requisitioned three stables for ponies for the grandchildren and a very old mare of mine.

The garden, however, was always going to be low-maintenance. I was busy with my design practice, and also still looking after the Helmingham gardens. However, I do now realize that no garden is completely low-maintenance. And, as my passion is not to be subdued, this one is growing, just little by little.

A wide grass verge surrounds the house and I have planted hornbeam blocks all around. Yes, we are doing quite well on low maintenance so far. I have recently cultivated a stretch of grass that was waist-high with weeds, clearing it and planting huge shrub roses 'Nevada' and 'Golden Showers', with acid-green foliage plants.

One approaches the house by a drive curling around the big barn and in front of it I have planted eight *Prunus* 'Shirotae', underplanted with blocks of white narcissi and blue scillas, followed on by clouds of *Oenothera* (syn. *Gaura*) *lindheimeri*, which flower from June to November. In front of that, we have a recently planted osmanthus hedge, starting low and sweeping up to meet the surrounding hedges.

So what was I going to do with Michael and Terrie's rose garden gone to pot? I was experimenting with designing on my iPad coming home on a train from a client visit and found I was beginning to draw shapes which echoed the herringbone pattern of the gables of the house. It came to me that it might be fun to have wavy hedges of *Osmanthus* x *burkwoodii* interspersed with varieties of lavender which flower from June to October. Simple, I thought. Osmanthus is cut once a year, the same with lavender, and then there is only a little weeding and, the mowing of the paths. So the beds were laid out, and I put in eight varieties of lavender divided into four large beds with a grass path up the middle and one across and some steps to a decking area from where I launch myself into the moat for a swim.

I knew there had to be a central feature, but the right idea had not yet materialized. However, during an art exhibition in the barn, I was very taken with a sculpture of a horse's head by Tom Hiscocks, and in an impulsive moment I bought it. I have not regretted the impulse and the horse's head now stands in a square pool with two triangular beds of box and lavender. It is an intriguing piece.

So this garden (once we had finally got rid of the thistles) is now very low maintenance and gets little attention – and, importantly, needs very little watering.

In front of the house was the original narrow flower border. I have widened this and made it a lot chunkier. Here I have made a herbaceous border and it is just long enough to keep me busy but not so much as to cause a nervous breakdown. The colour of the house is a pinky brown, called, rather surprisingly, Suffolk pink (but I did alter the colour a bit to make it softer). The colours of the border are cream and white, silver, blue, purple and dark red. I have planted lots of tulips here, with alliums, and I nick a few annuals from leftovers at Helmingham and grow a tiny amount in my minuscule greenhouse.

To the side of the house is a small enclosed garden with a huge chestnut tree. Here I planted spring flowers, with shade-loving plants around the outside. In the middle are several large shrubs and small trees. Hellebores, lamium, foxgloves, hostas, euphorbias, pulmonarias, brunnera, epimediums and anemones abound, with a few roses, daphnes and hydrangeas. The trees in the middle are a *Heptacodium miconoides*, *Malus* 'JohnDownie', *Carpinusfangiana*, *Sorbus wardii* and liquidambars.

OPPOSITE: Sculpture of a horse's head by Tom Hiscocks
RIGHT: My garden furniture on the moat terrace
BELOW: The Lavender Garden, showing how it was designed to complement the architecture of the house
OVERLEAF: The horse's head is the central feature of the Lavender Garden

This leads through to the orchard, which Tim has now cut through with winding mown paths. It overlooks the village and church below.

At the back of the house on the west side I have created a woodland garden, where the largest blackberry bush in Suffolk had taken over. We cleared a lot of laurel, which was originally planted for windbreaks, and I have put in lots of snowdrops and woodlanders, with a beautiful *Malus transitoria* in the centre between two lovely large cherries. There are remnants of shrubs that we planted when we were first here and also of those that my brother- and sister-in-law had put in. Leading back from this is a strip of woodland that we have now cleared, and I trimmed a path down to an open glade where we can picnic and make dens. (My grandsons follow my obsession with a machete, and are very taken with my battery-operated saw.)

There is a small natural pond which has enormous ash trees that still look healthy, and there are irises and water-loving plants. Here also there are two magnificent 'Tai-haku' cherry trees, given to my sister-in-law by her mother. They are now huge, and we sit under this vast canopy of white flowers in the spring.

I have my fire pit in this area, but otherwise it is a large rough lawn overlooking stunning Suffolk countryside, only separated from the field by a deep ditch. I have planted several trees in this area, including a fastigiate *Koelreuteria paniculata*, a *Nothofagus antarctica*, a gleditsia, a catalpa, two *Sorbus alnifolia* 'Red Bird' and three *Quercus palustris*.

On the far side, where the heather garden once presided (and was sensibly removed by my in-laws), I have planted silver birch in a glade, and an existing osmanthus has been cloud-pruned and underplanted by a mass of ornamental grasses with many varieties of asters. This bit of the garden is thick with daffodils, cowslips, primroses, naturalized bluebells and ferns, and leads into a wooded area with native trees and cow

OPPOSITE: The front border, with *Veronicastrum virginicum* 'Lavendelturm' and climbing rose 'Mermaid'
ABOVE: The grass and aster border, with *Betula utilis* subsp. *jacquemontii* and the *Crouching Man* sculpture by Laurence Edwards

parsley. Fritillaries are naturalizing there, and a little path leads you over a bridge to come out the far side.

The house looks out on to ancient grass meadows and the bottom meadow is where Tim has cultivated cowslips. It is a sight to behold: a mass of pale yellow greets you as you enter it. (Officially named the House Meadow, it did not earn its nickname of the Cowslip Meadow for nothing!)

There is still a lot to do and I feel that all the areas of horticulture need tying in and to work with each other – which is part of the fun of gardening. I always feel so good when I am out working in the garden – and now it is officially recognized that horticulture is immensely beneficial to our health and mental well-being.

When I am weeding or deadheading, or doing some other simple task, perhaps sitting on the mower, it is then that my mind goes into freefall. It can go anywhere and so often my best and most inspired ideas come while I am in the garden and on autopilot. Alternatively, my head can go into rest mode and I just go snip-snip-snip and come back into the house refreshed, perhaps tired, but always happy.

My dearest wish would be that more people could understand the huge benefits of gardening, whether in a large garden or a window box; and that the government in charge, whoever it may be, would recognize the garden's healing power.

THE HELMINGHAM COLLECTION

Having now settled down at Framsden, I have begun to build up the range of garden furniture that I started designing at Helmingham.

There is really very little on the market in the way of high-end garden furniture that you can leave out all year round, that is not too costly, and that is British-made. So the Helmingham Collection was born. It is available in two materials: the finer one in mild steel and the more sturdy in aluminium. Both are galvanized and powder-coated in any of the RAL colours.

We have designed dining tables and chairs, garden sofas, armchairs and coffee tables with our distinctive fret design taken from the Tollemache family crest. We can make up to any measurements and can arrange for piped cushions to be made to fit. We can also offer a bespoke service for any additional pieces.

This elegant range, perfect for any town or country garden, can be seen on my website (www.xa-tollemache.co.uk)

THE HELMINGHAM ROSE SUPPORT

In 1984 I designed a new support system for my old-fashioned shrub roses In the gardens at Helmingham. Consisting of one central pole 1.8 metres/ 6 feet in length, 10 metal stakes and an 18-metre/60-foot coil of wire, the Helmingham Rose Support provides an informal and natural structure for old-fashioned roses, which tend to be lax and sprawling. Even after heavy rainfall the rose still retains its shape. What is more, the Support also encourages shrub roses to produce a greater profusion of blooms, as tying down the shoots enables flowering all along the stem.

To get the maximum benefit from the Support, shrub roses should be at least three years old. There is no upper age limit – all roses of three years or older should benefit. My Rose Supports have now been in position for thirty-five years and have never needed to be replaced.

The Helmingham Rose Support system is available in kit form. Again, for details see my website, www.xa-tollemache.co.uk.

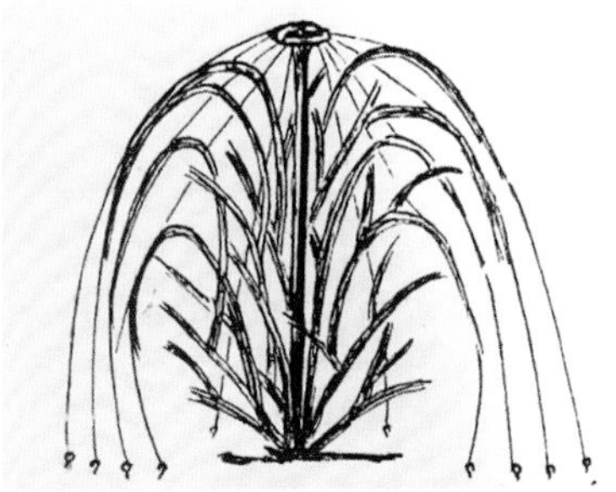

BELOW LEFT: Table and chairs from the Helmingham Collection in our garden at Framsden
BELOW: Shrub roses 'Marchesa Boccella', 'Ispahan' and 'Mme Plantier', all showing the effect created by the Helmlngham Rose Support (above)

GARDENS

Hayward House, Berkshire, 1996
Château de la Roque, Gascony, 1996
Ginge Manor, Oxfordshire, 1996
Bighton House, Hampshire, 1996–2021
Chelsea Flower Show, London, 1997 (Gold Medal)
Dunbeath Castle, Caithness, 1998
Hampstead, London, 1998
Chester Street, London, 1998
Balfour Mews, Mayfair, London, 1998
Hertwood Terrace, Chiswick, London, 1998
Wilton House, Wiltshire, 1998–2017
Easton Grey, Wiltshire, 1999
Brantham Glebe, Suffolk, 1999
Castle Hill, Devon, 2000–2009
Chartley, Staffordshire, 2001
Castle Heaton, Northumberland, 2001
Chelsea Flower Show, London, 2001 (Silver-Gilt Medal)
Egeskov Castle, Denmark, c. 2002
Chelsea Flower Show, London, 2003 (Silver-Gilt Medal)
Princeton, New Jersey, 2003
No 1 Knightsbridge, London, 2004
Crowe Hall, Suffolk, 2005
Albermarle House, Virginia, 2005
Christchurch Mansions, Ipswich, 2005
Civettaia, Italy, 2005
Brookhurst, Massachusetts, 2006
Crows Hall, Suffolk, 2006
Bolesworth Castle, Cheshire, 2008
Cholmondeley Castle, Cheshire, 2008
Elton Hall, Northamptonshire 2008
Sapiston, Suffolk, 2008
Egerton Terrace, London, 2009
Foxhole Cottage, Suffolk, 2009
Orchard House, Cornwall, 2009
Tunstall Hall, Suffolk, 2009
Waterstock, Oxford, 2009
Bays Farm, Suffolk, 2009
Iscoyd Park, Shropshire, 2009–2020
Manor Farm, Norfolk, 2010
Birchgrove House, Sussex, 2010
Grange Farm, Suffolk, 2010
The Grove, Suffolk, 2010
The Old Rectory, Wilton, Wiltshire, 2010
Fittocks Stud, Newmarket, Suffolk, 2012
Town house in Aldeburgh, Suffolk, 2012
Ashdon House, Saffron Walden, Essex, 2012
Oakley Park, Suffolk, 2012
Saxstead House, Suffolk, 2012
Green Farm, Suffolk, 2012–2013
Somerleyton Hall, Suffolk, 2013
Darmsden Hall, Suffolk, 2013
Denston Hall, Suffolk, 2013
Vincent Square, London, 2013
Aspell House, Suffolk, 2014
Hitcham Hall, Suffolk, 2014
Beaulieu Lodge, Hampshire, 2014
Tetworth, Berkshire, 2014
Bell House, Newmarket, Suffolk, 2015
Brynmaer Road, London, 2015
Donhead Lodge, Dorset, 2015
The Garden House, Devon, 2016
RHS Hyde Hall, Essex, 2016–18
Rhug, Wales, 2017
Framsden Hall, Suffolk, 2017 onwards
The Hay Bays, Cheshire, 2018
Houghton Hall, Norfolk, 2018
Stone House, Suffolk, 2018–2021
Silverley House, Berkshire, 2019
Newnhams Rough, Sussex, 2019
Dorfold Hall, Cheshire, 2020
Hyde Mill, Gloucestershire, 2020
Slough Hall, Suffolk, 2020
Tunstall Cottage, Suffolk, 2020
Launceston Place, London, 2020
Benham Park, Berkshire, 2021
Bramfield Hall, Suffolk, 2021
The Jockey Club, Newmarket, Suffolk, 2021

INDEX

Page numbers in italics refer to illustrations

ACKNOWLEDGEMENTS

My thanks must go to Jo Christian of Pimpernel Press, who first encouraged me to write a book back in 2016. And to the marvellous staff of Pimpernel, especially Managing Director Gail Lynch, who has been equally encouraging, Art Director Becky Clarke, who produced the beautiful design, and Picture Editor Sue Gladstone, who was so brilliantly helpful in sorting out the photographs. Thanks also to Tony Lord, who not only compiled the index, but also checked plant names throughout the book. I want to thank Tim, my husband, for his encouragement in my garden design business and his constant love and support. Our children, who unfailingly encourage me, and the grandchildren, who inspire me.

The people who have helped us create a garden at Helmingham that is worthy of writing about: the gardening team with their hard work and enthusiasm, positivity, and huge horticultural knowledge and wisdom. I must particularly emphasize the invaluable support and hard work of Roy Balaam.

In the office, Alison, Katy and Lynda have endlessly typed up documents, and different versions of the text, as well as researching the photos, all without complaint.

My friend David Campbell, who set me off on this unknown path of writing, and introduced me to my wonderful editor, Eleo Carson, who so skilfully guided me along it.

I would also like to thank all the people who helped make the Hall into a wonderful family home. David Mlinaric, who achieved such a miraculous transformation, and the teams who supported that. Our clerk of the works, Rob Parmenter, who was always there to repair, mend and build, either in the garden or the house. And all our helpers, who ensured that everything got done (with a lot of elbow grease and good humour).

Thanks to Max Hastings, who gave me the commission to do a garden at the Chelsea Flower Show, which put me on a more professional platform. Thank you, too, to the Royal Horticultural Society, for inviting me to join Council and the various Committees, various where I have learned an enormous amount.

A huge debt of thanks is owed to my assistant, Jane Bailey. Between us we have created and worked on more than fifty gardens. With her amazing computer skills she produces impressive drawings from my rough hand-drawn designs. She is also invaluable in sourcing plants, arranging deliveries and answering queries. Also thanks to my previous wonderful helpers, Roger Balmer, Lucy Roberts, Lucy Readman and Camilla Trusted. And to my fantastic contractors, Jeff Hewitt, Chris McDaniel , Daren Revell and Conker Landscapes, as well as to the private teams of the various gardens.

Then, of course, to all the garden owners, for so generously giving over their gardens for me to design, and for their support and enthusiasm Working with them all gave me such pleasure and we have almost invariably become friends as a result. Whether their gardens are large and open to the public, or smaller and private spaces, they have all been interesting and each has had their special point. It is a pity that there is not room to show all of their gardens, but my gratitude goes to all those clients who have put their trust in me.

And to all the photographers who have taken such great pictures of Helmingham and the other gardens: especially to Marcus Harpur, Allan Pollok-Morris, Anthony Cullen and Chris Reeve – but, absolutely, to them all.

My admiration for Fergus Garrett goes back a long way. I could see, on my various visits to Great Dixter over the years, that Fergus was taking the garden up to further levels of brilliance, innovation and understanding (way above the rest of us). To have him put my beloved Helmingham in the same bracket as Dixter is very humbling, and I cannot thank him enough for his kind words.

Lastly, my thanks to Helmingham, which first taught me to garden and then always greeted me with its warmth and friendliness as I drove back after a spell away.

PICTURE CREDITS

The publishers have made every effort to contact holders of copyright works. Any copyright holders we have been unable to reach are invited to contact the publishers so that a full acknowledgement may be given in subsequent editions. For permission to reproduce the images below, the publishers would like to thank the following:

Jane Bailey: 143
Julia Bickham: 80/81
Simon Buck: 70 above, 72 left
Conkerlandscapes.com: 151
Anthony Cullen: 126, 127, 128/9, 130, 131, 132, 133, 134, 135, 136, 137, 138, 139, 140, 141, 148, 149, 150, 152, 154, 155, 156, 157, 159, 160, 161, 163, 164/5, 166, 167, 168 below
Katy Day: 66 right
Jill Fenwick: 85
Jerry Harpur /GAP Photos Ltd.: 34 below left
Marcus Harpur /GAP Photos Ltd.: opposite contents page, 12, 14, 28, 29, 31, 32/3, 34 above, 43, 51, 52 below, 58, 59 below, 60, 62/3, 64 left, 65, 70 below right, 72/3 centre, 75, 76 left & centre, 169 below
Tim Kahane/Trigger Air: 26/7
Andrew Lawson: 84, 87, 122, 123
Marianne Majerus: 30, 77
William Pembroke: 120, 121, 125
Allan Pollok-Morris: 22, 36, 37, 38 left, 38/9, 40, 54 below, 67, 88, 89, 91, 92, 93, 102, 103, 105, 106, 107, 108, 109, 110, 111, 112, 113, 114, 115, 116, 117, 118,
Private Collection: 11, 13, 21, 82 left, 95, 124
RHS: 144, 145
RHS/Chris Gorman: 142, 146, 147
Chris Reeve: 24/5, 34/5 below, 42, 45 left, 45 below right, 46 above left, 52 above, 53, 54 above & centre, 61 below left, 64 right, 66 left, 70 below left, 76 right, 78, 79
Ellen Rooney: 61 above, 61 below right
Mollie Salisbury: 57, 59 above
Lindsey Saunders: title page, 8, 48/9, 83
Brenda Skinner: 94, 96, 97, 98, 99, 100, 101
Gary Summers, SMD Photography: half-title page, 18, 23, 50, 69
James Sumpter: 16/17
Tim Tollemache: 41, 44, 45 above right, 46 above right, below left & below right, 56 above, 73 right, 153, 162
Xa Tollemache: 47, 56 below, 90, 119, 169 above
Bernie Totten: 168 above & centre
© Mark Ward Media: 82 right